EMPLOYEES FIRST,
CUSTOMERS SECOND

EMPLOYEES FIRST,

CUSTOMERS
SECOND

turning conventional management upside down

VINEET NAYAR

Harvard Business Press

Boston, Massachusetts

Library of Congress Cataloging-in-Publication Data

Nayar, Vineet.
  Employees first, customers second : turning conventional management
upside down / by Vineet Nayar.
    p. cm.
  ISBN 978-1-4221-3906-6 (hbk. : alk. paper) 1. Management—
Employee participation. 2. Corporate culture. 3. Organizational
change. 4. Customer relations. 5. HCL Technologies—
Management—Case studies. I. Title.
  HD5650.N375 2010
  658.3'152—dc222

                                                        2009050642

Contents

Foreword: A Practical Narrative

It is not very often we get a firsthand account from a CEO about how he transformed his organization from a slow decline to an engine of vitality and growth. That is what Vineet Nayar provides in this detailed first-person narrative of his company's journey over the last five years.

The book offers three perspectives. First, we get a glimpse of a major transformation from Vineet's viewpoint as the CEO—his doubts, his process of discovery, the validation of his ideas, and the building of consensus. Second, we witness the migration in his thinking about management from the old to the new—from a focus on the traditional hierarchical structure to one that decentralizes power, responsibility, and accountability for value creation. Third, we explore the cultural prerequisites for this approach to management—the need for honesty, transparency, trust, and dialogue at all levels in the organization.

Most important, Vineet recognizes that today the asset base of an organization increasingly resides in the talent and creativity of its employees. Knowledge-based businesses, especially, depend on excited teams of individuals who are eager to take on one challenging task after another and to act as custodians of the tacit knowledge in the organization. To manage them—especially Gen Y employees, and particularly in global organizations—requires a new set of capabilities. Vineet's story shows how a company can focus on its value creators—the frontline employees—to achieve remarkable growth and profits.

In a time when we are witnessing a rapid shift from traditional manufacturing to knowledge-based companies—and, as a result, a transformation of the work of managers and of management practice—this book raises important philosophical questions. Is there inherent value in every employee—in his or her knowledge, creativity, commitment to tasks, and capacity to collaborate? To create the most value for customers, should we focus on how employees are empowered? Do employees, in short, make a difference?

Vineet answers these questions in this easy-to-read, first-person account. It is a narrative of organizational transformation and a practical guide for managers who wish to achieve similar results, as well as a story of the personal transformation of a CEO. I recommend it wholeheartedly.

—C. K. Prahalad

Paul and Ruth McCracken Distinguished
University Professor

Ross School of Business
University of Michigan

Introduction

Not long ago, on a flight from New York to Frankfurt, I got talking with the passenger seated next to me. He asked what I did, and I said that I was CEO of a global information technology (IT) services company. When I asked him the same question, he said he was a retired race-car driver.

During the flight, we chatted on and off, talking about our lives and professions. As we sipped a glass of wine before dinner, he told me about an incident from his past. It seems he had been in the middle of a race when his brakes failed. He asked if I had ever had that experience. "No," I said. "What did you do?"

"What do you think my options were?" he asked.

I thought of a number of possibilities, but I really had no idea.

"Most drivers do one of two things," he said. "First, they try to get the brakes to work. Or, second, they slow down. The first option distracts the driver and puts him at risk of a crash. The second option makes him a hazard to other drivers and also puts him at risk of a crash."

"So what should you do?" I asked.

"Speed up," he said. "Accelerate past the other cars and then take whatever action is necessary."

I have no idea if that strategy really works in a race or if it was just the wine talking. And I have yet to come across another race-car driver I could ask about it. But I did wonder why that option hadn't occurred to me.

As I thought about it, another incident came to my mind. I had recently bumped into a childhood friend whom I hadn't seen in twenty-five years. I couldn't help but blurt out, "Wow. You look so different. I can't believe it!"

Well, why wouldn't he look different? Why did I react with such shock? Why don't I feel the same shock when I look at myself in the mirror? After all, I've changed just as much as my friend has.

Maybe it has to do with the way the brain is wired to deal with change. When the brakes fail, the change is instant and you have no choice but to try to think of options for action. But with gradual change, like aging, you don't really notice it until something forces you to.

The race-car driver's story struck me so powerfully, I guess, because I was in the middle of a race at the time, a race to transform our business, and I was following exactly the strategy my fellow passenger had described: speed up to get past the competitors and find open room to maneuver.

Of course, I didn't think of it quite that way then, in the spring of 2005. I just knew that our company, HCL Technologies (HCLT), was in a tough spot and that we had to do something fast or we were in danger of being out of the race altogether. I had been the head of the company for only a short time and was still trying to grasp what it meant to lead such a large enterprise. I had run a smaller, entrepreneurial unit of HCL, called Comnet, that I had founded, and now I was leading one of the five major IT services companies based in India. The company had thirty thousand employees, operations in eighteen countries, yearly revenue of about $700 million, and a healthy compound annual growth rate (CAGR) of about 30 percent over the previous five years.

But behind these fairly impressive numbers lay a difficult reality. HCLT was like my childhood friend who suddenly looked old. Once one of India's corporate stars, HCLT was growing more slowly than the market leader in its industry (a company which had achieved a 50 percent CAGR over the last five years) and slower than its immediate rivals, losing market share and falling behind in mindshare, too.

Still, the HCL name was legendary in India. The company was founded in 1976 in a *barsaati*, the Indian equivalent of a garage start-up in the United States, by a group of young entrepreneurs led by Shiv Nadar, a pioneer of the

Indian IT industry and today one of India's most respected business leaders.

I joined the company in 1985 straight out of college when the company was in its infancy, with less than $10 million in sales. I had a dream of joining a small company and helping to make it big, and Shiv had a powerful vision for the computing industry, as well as an ability to think beyond the obvious, which I found fascinating.

The dream largely came true. The worldwide IT industry took off, just as Shiv foresaw that it would, and India's technology companies exploded with it. HCL became a leader in its chosen businesses and markets, growing from about $10 million to $5 billion over a twenty-five-year period led by HCL Technologies along with another unit of the group, HCL Infosystems. For many of those years, HCL was the leader of the race, holding the number one position ahead of its Indian peers. It was among the first to introduce many technology and service innovations to the world, and those innovations, combined with an entrepreneurial culture, attracted the best and brightest to work at HCL.

From 2000 to 2005, however, HCLT had fallen back in the pack. Somehow, we didn't see that we were slowing down (even if 30 percent annual growth doesn't sound slow) and that our competitors were racing past us. Why the blind spot? Perhaps we felt satisfied with the growth we had accomplished. Perhaps we believed we were doing the best we could do. Perhaps we were offering the wrong mix of services for the changed marketplace.

This happens to companies all too often. Unless the company becomes obsessed with constant change for the better, gradual change for the worse usually goes unnoticed. We have seen this happen to once-great companies around the world. It could happen to yours, too; it may already be happening.

So, when do you need to make the decision to change? When the time comes, there will be many questions to ask yourself: Why have we decided to change? What level of change should our organization aspire to? What companies should we benchmark against? How will we go about making the change? How much risk can we tolerate in our change efforts?

One fine day, we at HCLT (now a family of fifty-five thousand people and around $2.5 billion in revenues) made the decision to change, and this book tells the story of our fascinating journey of self-discovery and how we accomplished our transformation through a unique approach:

- We forced ourselves to look in the mirror and recognize that we had changed for the worse.

- We stepped on the accelerator and surged forward, moving from a position far back in the pack to one of leadership with the fastest growth in our industry—about 3X revenue growth in four years. (We were one of the few companies in the world to grow during the 2008–2009 recession.)

- We changed from a workplace with high attrition and low attraction to being named the Number One Best Employer in India and Best Employer in Asia and the United Kingdom.

- We stopped spouting the same old business bromides and became a thought leader and innovator, named by *BusinessWeek* as one of the top five emerging companies to watch, and described by *Fortune* as having "the world's most modern management."

- We gained attention and praise with coverage in major business publications throughout the world and were taught as a case study at Harvard Business School, not only for what we have accomplished but also for how we have done so.

The last point is a critical one: any transformation journey requires innovation both in *what* you do and in *how* you do it. The business world is largely focused on the *what* of the strategy—new products, new propositions, new markets—and pays far less attention to *how* a business runs its teams and companies. In our experience, the difference in the *how* offers the greatest opportunity to drive transformation and accelerated growth. So, although I do describe the *what* of our strategy, because it did play a part in the transformation, I speak much more about the *how*, which is really the most interesting and valuable part of our story.

We call the *how* approach *Employees First, Customers Second*, or EFCS. The conventional wisdom, of course, says that companies must always put the *customer* first. In any services business, however, the true value is created in the interface between the customer and the employee. So, by putting employees first, you can bring about fundamental change in the way a company creates and delivers unique value for its customers and differentiates itself from its competitors. Through a combination of engaged employees and accountable management, a company can create extraordinary value for itself, its customer, and the individuals involved in both companies.

Thus, when a company puts its employees first, the customer actually does ultimately come first and gains the greatest benefit, but in a far more transformative way than through traditional "customer care" programs and the like.

EFCS involves a number of specific practices and actions and a framework of implementation that can create outstanding results. It is also a "thinking journey" that is constantly evolving, with new ideas and initiatives taking shape along the way.

In this book, we describe four phases of the EFCS journey that we progressed through at HCLT, although the phases may be better thought of as components, because each of the four tends to be revisited in different configurations and sequences as new initiatives unfold. What's more, there may well be a fifth or sixth component that others, outside our company, have identified and that we might explore in the future.

I have written this book to provoke thought and discussion about the concept of EFCS rather than to capture all the facts about the HCLT transformation. So think of this book as a description of the many experiments, debates, and unconventional ideas we generated in the course of one journey, during one period, for one specific company and its people. This specific journey is one that others can learn from, adapt, and apply in a thousand ways to their own situations, in any team, company, industry, or culture. Because this is not intended to be a journalistic narrative of our company, I have changed the names of some of the people who appear in the book, although they are all based on real people, and some of the scenes and conversations are recollected from memory, rather than taken from transcripts or detailed notes, so they should be considered as representative. I have indicated in the text where names have been changed.

The book is structured around the four phases, as outlined in the following sections.

Mirror Mirror: Creating the Need for Change

Where does one begin a change? By looking in the mirror. Why does the fundamental truth of a business situation escape so many managers? I don't know, but I know that it does. In 2005, we had an option to keep going as we were or to change. We chose to force ourselves to face the reality of our trailing position. However, doing so once is not enough. We learned that it is necessary to look in the mirror every day and, when you do, to look for the things you *don't* like about what you see, rather than just focusing on the pleasing things, those attributes that your marketing slogans already feature.

At the same time, you must create a picture of what could be, if you were to change. This future image is what I call the *romance of tomorrow*, and that's what motivates people to press the accelerator to the floor when logic tells them to step on the brake. Chapter 1 describes some of the discussions and debates we had, and some of the actions we took, so that we all could begin to see the need for change at HCLT. Even so, although an awareness of the need is absolutely necessary, it's not the same as making the change itself.

Trust Through Transparency: Creating a Culture of Change

Once you have created the need for change, there is often a significant gap between the intent to change and the actual act of changing. Chapter 2 explains that one reason for this gap is a lack of trust among employees and

management, a condition that is, unfortunately, quite common today. To transform a company, people must align
themselves and work together toward one goal, but this will
not happen without a culture of trust.

There are many ways to build trust, and many other
writers have discussed them. At HCLT, we focused on
one specific trust-building action: pushing the envelope
of transparency. As we did, we found that most people
within the organization know very well what's wrong with
a company, sometimes even before management does or, at
least, before management is willing to admit it. When you
bring this information out into the open and make the
challenges public, employees feel included. They start to see
that the problems of the company are really their problems,
too, not just those of the management. They realize that
if management is willing to share important information,
even the bad stuff, and encourages open conversation about
the facts, its intentions can be trusted. Very quickly, you will
start seeing some positive action at the grassroots level even
before management can decide on actions and solutions.
Many times, we saw employees start working on problems
without being asked to do so.

Tough times will test the courage of management's
convictions and its commitment to following the new
path. We were tested during the recession of 2008–2009,
and we stayed on course. This created tremendous trust
between management and employees—trust that benefitted the company when we emerged from the hard times

and went for the next level of performance. Other companies, which had taken hasty actions designed to improve short-term results, find themselves facing a difficult challenge when they ask their employees to fully engage as the companies try to grow post recession. I expect that we will see more evidence of this as we follow the performance of some of these companies in the coming years.

Inverting the Organizational Pyramid: Building a Structure for Change

Even when people see the need for change, after a culture of trust has been created, and employees have started taking actions toward positive change, structural flaws can still get in the way of optimal results and it's important to remember that the success of a single initiative is not the same as sustainable change. HCLT and many other companies around the world try to conduct new-age business with centuries-old structures—hierarchies and matrixes that many thought leaders consider obsolete.

At HCLT, our biggest problem with the organization structure was that it did not support the people in what we call the *value zone*: the place where value is truly created for customers. In a services company in a knowledge economy, this zone lies in the interface between the customer and the employee. In traditional companies, the value zone is often buried deep inside the hierarchy and the people who create the most value in the company work there. Paradoxically, these value-creators are almost always accountable to bosses and managers—typically located at the top of the pyramid or in the so-called "enabling functions"—who do not directly contribute to the value zone. But, because these "superiors" hold formal authority and the value-creators are accountable to them, they occupy a zone of power.

So, to shift our focus to the value zone, we turned the organization upside down and made management and managers, including those in enabling functions (such as human resources, finance, training, and others), accountable to those who create value, not just the other way around. Without making these structural shifts, change is much more difficult, if not impossible. And only by making adjustments to the organizational structure does the change become sustainable and able to outlast the leader who initiated the transformation. Chapter 3 gives important details about inverting the organizational pyramid.

Recasting the Role of the CEO: Transferring the Responsibility for Change

There has been a lot of debate about the role of leadership, particularly after so many companies got into such trouble during the recession and even as whole countries have struggled under poor leadership. Leadership is fundamental to a company, and the role of leadership is perhaps the most difficult to define in companies that compete in a knowledge economy. One of the structural flaws of traditional management systems is that the leader holds too much power. That prevents the organization from becoming democratized and the energy of the employees from being released. If your objective is to create sustainable change and to prevent your company from periodically falling out of the race, you must think carefully about the role of the *office* of the CEO and not just the role of the person who holds the job at the moment.

During this phase, I learned that as CEO, or as any leader or manager, you must stop thinking of yourself as the only source of change. You must avoid the urge to answer every question or provide a solution to every problem. Instead, you must start asking questions, seeing others as the source of change, and transferring ownership of the organization's growth to the next generation of leaders who are closer to the value zone. Only in this way can you begin to create a company that is self-run and self-governed, one in which employees feel like the owners, are excited by their work, and constantly focus on change and disruptive innovation at the very heart of the value zone. Indeed, as I explain in chapter 4, the greatest impact of EFCS is that it unleashes the power of the many and loosens the stranglehold of the few, thus increasing the speed and quality of innovation and decision making where it matters most—in the value zone—every day.

Find Understanding in Misunderstanding: Renewing the Cycle of Change

It is easy to misunderstand the intent and the methods of EFCS, and in chapter 5, I discuss the various objections to our approach that I have heard:

- It will not work in difficult times.

- It is not necessary in good times.

- Customers will never see the value.

- It requires large-scale initiatives.

- It does not improve a company's performance.

In fact, the practices we employed at HCLT, and those that you might employ at your company, bring real value to customers in good times and bad, do not require massive initiatives or expenditures, and have a marked positive effect on corporate performance.

That is because the practices should really be seen as catalysts of positive change. I often call the practices—or, interchangeably, the people who originate them—*blue ocean droplets*, after the book *Blue Ocean Strategy*, by W. Chan Kim and Renée Mauborgne, because these small ideas can create an ocean of change and enable a company to enter an entirely new performance zone, no matter what its current situation may be.

Catalysts are simple actions, rather than elaborate programs of organizational change that plod on for years and years, and they can help transform a locked-up culture into one that can constantly evolve. Sometimes the catalysts don't create change or can lead to unexpected secondary effects. That's OK, because our misunderstandings always lead to deeper understanding. As external conditions change, the thinking journey begins again.

Your Own Journey

The four phases or components I describe in the book may sound as if they present difficult, even insurmountable, challenges. But it takes just one catalyst idea, one droplet, to begin to overcome them. Many other leaders, who have led transformations far more sweeping than ours at HCLT, understood the power of catalysts. I think, for example, of Mahatma Gandhi's famous Dandi March; he walked to the sea to make salt as a protest against the British government and their monopoly on salt production in India—a small action that led to large-scale uprising in the country.

I do not believe that the catalysts we employed are necessarily the ones that you should employ in your company or that the way we achieved a transformation at HCLT is the way you might transform your company or your teams. You must make your own journey. Your thinking phases are likely to be different from ours. Your catalysts may be different, too.

One thought, however, should be fundamental to all our journeys: turn conventional management upside down by putting employees first.

CHAPTER ONE

Mirror Mirror

Creating the Need for Change

To begin at the beginning.

In early 2005, the employees of HCLT were in a celebratory mood. The company had surpassed $700 million in annual revenue. It had a good track record of growth. Employees had plenty of stories to tell about themselves, the company, our innovative products, and their long-standing relationships with customers. Most people in the company were feeling good.

A few, however, were looking at the flip side of the coin. HCLT was growing, yes, but not nearly as fast as the leaders in the IT services industry. And, despite its revenue growth, the company was actually losing market share. It was also rapidly losing mindshare outside India, because of gains other companies were making. And HCLT had a people problem, too, since some of its most talented employees were leaving to work for competitors.

While many observers thought HCLT was a race car leading the field, a few saw that the brakes could fail at any moment and the vehicle could easily crash into a wall. What was the reality of the situation? Which observation was true?

This was the fundamental question HCLT faced—the same one that many other companies had to confront in 2008 during the depths of the recession. Is the company in enough danger that it should attempt to transform itself before it's too late? Or should it just ride out the storm and hope for things to get better?

As it happened, I became the one to ask those questions. In late 2004, when I was the CEO of HCL Comnet, an entrepreneurial unit of HCL, the president of HCL Technologies fell into poor health. Soon thereafter, I got a call from Shiv Nadar, chairman and founder of the company.

"Vineet," he said. "I want you to consider coming on board to head HCLT."

I was not sure I wanted the job. I was happy at Comnet, the company that I, along with my team, had built from the ground up into a global enterprise. Comnet was seen as a pioneer and a dominant leader in remote infrastructure management, a fast-growing segment of the

IT services industry. We had created an entrepreneurial environment and built successful operations in eleven countries; our company was growing faster than its industry peers. I had been successful in creating a start-up, but running a large, well-established company with a legacy business would be a very different ball game. Moreover, I had always thought that small is beautiful and the energy, speed, and innovation in companies like Comnet (around $500 million in revenue today) kept my adrenalin pumping and I did not want to give that environment up.

I guess I had brought the situation on myself. I had been a vocal critic of some of the strategies being employed at HCLT and had often expressed to Shiv that the company was not at the front of the race but, in fact, rapidly losing speed. But I had never said that *I* wanted to climb into the driver's seat.

I politely declined Shiv's invitation to become president and thought that it would end there.

A few weeks later, he called and said, "Come to my house for dinner. Let's talk it over some more."

We had dinner, then discussed the issue well into the night. Shiv understood the changing forces driving the IT industry and the problems that HCLT faced. Having seen what we had accomplished at Comnet with a radical management style, he had concluded that HCLT could no longer operate in the traditional ways. I told him that it was just as likely that I would destroy HCLT as it was that

I would help transform it. Shiv has been a mentor and a close friend since I started Comnet in 1993, and in the end, it was impossible to say no to him.

"But," I said, "I must do it my way. I have to be free to adopt an unconventional approach."

"Of course," said Shiv.

And that was that. He didn't ask me exactly what that unconventional approach might be—which was a good thing, because I didn't know.

The Missing Starting Point

One of the joys of life is to watch your children as they learn new things.

I remember the first time my kids learned to hold a pencil. They would grab any kind of writing surface, put the point of the pencil to it, and draw a line. They were amazed by the magic of this instrument. After a lot of scribbling, they learned the art of drawing a straight line by connecting two dots. That simple action brought great pleasure and clarity to their thinking. And isn't that how we try to live our lives? We start at a defined point A and try to get to a defined point B.

So, as I prepared to become president of HCLT, I thought a great deal about where we were and where we wanted to go and tried to simplify our situation. I realized, with some surprise, that neither a point A nor a point B had been clearly defined. People had different views on where the company was (racing ahead or about to crash?), and nobody had clearly expressed where the company was headed or should be headed. It was evident that point A remained undefined—or that the company was still hanging on to a point A that had been defined, but long ago—because we had never really slowed down. It was just that our peers had sped ahead and were growing much faster than we were.

I looked around at other companies for a model of how we might change. The majority of them were quite clear about their point B. It was articulated in their statements of vision, mission, and goals. But, to my amazement, I realized that most of them had not defined their point A with equal clarity. They neglected this vital element in a fast-changing environment that very quickly can make a company's position obsolete. In most cases, the only definition of point A was in financial statements and other such basic data that gave only a rather limited and absolute view of the situation.

This puzzled me. Is it possible to make a plan to reach point B without understanding and agreeing on point A? I didn't think so. Can a child draw a line without first putting the point of the pencil at a distinct spot on the paper?

This thinking clarified the first step we needed to take: we had to define our point A and see how the truth had changed.

Changes in the Environment

A company's performance in relation to its peers is just one factor that defines its point A. It is equally important to look at the entire landscape of the industry in which you operate and to see how it is evolving. Often, the landscape has shifted so much that the original point A has fallen off the edge of the map.

For HCLT, the fundamental change in the landscape was that, over the previous five years, information technology had become more and more central to business strategy. Companies like Boeing, Dell, Amazon.com, and eBay had used technology to change the rules of the game so dramatically, they were actually playing a different game altogether, leaving their competitors to play catch-up or to drop out of the running completely.

In 2005, the influence of technology on business was exploding still further, with developments in telecommunications, Web services, and social media. Technology had become central not only to strategy within existing business models, but also to creating and sustaining entirely new models, from Li & Fung's reinvention of the global supply chain to Google's invention of a new online revenue model.

All of this change led to a dramatic rise in the importance of the position of chief information officer, (CIO). In the traditional hierarchy, the senior business leadership had always formulated strategy, operations people in the middle had converted strategy into a set of activities, and the IT executives at the bottom found ways to automate those activities to make them as efficient and cost-effective as possible. In this traditional model, the businesspeople rarely interacted with IT; they just directed.

Now, however, CIOs were expected to deliver faster, cheaper, and better processes that could help the companies differentiate themselves from their competitors and achieve the desired competitive advantage. The shift was so dramatic that a new career path opened, from CIO to CEO. Just a few years earlier, it would have been rare to see a CIO taking over as senior leader, but now it was becoming relatively common. David Bernauer, CIO of Walgreens, had become its CEO; Bruce Giesbrecht had moved from the CIO spot to CEO of Hollywood Entertainment; and five or six others had done the same. I believed that this phenomenon (which I like to call the "reincarnated CIO") signaled a very different future for enterprise IT and its leaders.

In the traditional IT organization, the CIO often acted as a competent caretaker. In the new intelligent enterprises, CIOs were expected to be proactive and to become agents of change, contributors to business agility, and managers of mission-critical operations. In other words, the main customers of HCLT—the CIOs and their staffs—were changing in very dramatic ways. Most of the industry was still struggling to come to terms with the pace of this change. Most HCLT employees had not yet fathomed the impact of it.

We had to make our employees see, very clearly, the truth of this new point A for the industry and that of our own point A within it.

Looking in the Mirror

The process we followed to get employees to see our situation at point A is one that eventually came to be called *Mirror Mirror*.

Mirror Mirror is a communications exercise that involves talking with employees throughout the organization about the truth as they see it and getting them to acknowledge the reality, the elephant in the room, that everyone essentially knows about but which has never been publicly acknowledged. It is a matter of getting the members of the organization to look at themselves in the mirror and describe carefully and truthfully what they see.

You cannot do this by sending out a memo and telling people to face up to reality. The process must be pursued, in person, face-to-face, together. So, the day I assumed my new role as president of HCLT, I got on a plane and spent the next two weeks visiting our facilities and talking with as many people at all levels of the company as I could.

I chose my first stop carefully: the city of Chennai, in the southern part of India, and the home of the HCLT Engineering Center. Much of our past success had come about because of the engineering services team's ability to spot emerging technology trends and to develop new products to meet them and get them to market ahead of competitors. I had worked there as a product manager earlier in my career and had been a part of many successful campaigns with the team. I knew that Chennai was the right place to start.

On the first day of my Mirror Mirror journey, I landed in Chennai, drove to the main facility, and, within a few minutes of arriving, began a session with about five hundred members of the engineering services team. I talked honestly about how I saw our current situation—my definition of our point A—and articulated the themes that I would stress over and over again during the following weeks.

- HCLT had lost its competitive edge because it had become tolerant of gradual change that did not match the rapid change of the industry, and, worse, it had come to see that pace as acceptable progress.

- The company could, however, crash any day and had a very limited amount of time to prevent such a disaster.

- The only way to prevent a disaster was to accelerate, move faster, and transform the company and the way it operated.

After my remarks, I paused for reactions. There weren't many comments. It was as if I had spoken the unspeakable and there was too much shock and hurt to allow for conversation. The pride we take in our work and in our past can make it difficult to hear the truth, let alone accept it. There were a few questions about what we would do now and what it all meant. Many of these questions, I couldn't answer. "I don't have all the answers yet," I told them. "I may never have the answers. They will have to come from you." This confused people even more. How could I tell them we had to change, without telling them exactly how?

Years later, some members of the engineering services team who had been in that session told me that they had taken my comments very personally and had been hurt by them. I could see the hurt at the time, but I knew it was necessary to point out the elephant in the room and for them to start thinking about it. Without the participation of the employees and their agreement on point A, we would never be able to reach point B.

All Aboard?

I left Chennai wondering how this would all turn out. Within a week, I was in the United States, visiting our many offices there. Within two weeks, I had been to London, Frankfurt, and Tokyo and had returned to Bangalore and Delhi. I had talked with thousands of employees, customers, and partners. In these conversations, I made the same remarks over and over, heard many of the same questions and comments, saw the same hurt and confusion.

As I met with people throughout the company and looked out over the faces of the employees in the meetings, an image from my childhood often came to mind. When I was a boy, our family sometimes traveled by train together. We would rush to the station and wait for the carriages to arrive. When the train finally pulled in and came to a halt, the conductor would step onto the platform and call out in his booming voice, "All aboard!" There was no hesitation among the waiting crowd. They would all surge forward, hoping to get a seat. I always loved to hear the conductor's call and to see what an immediate response it brought.

In those early meetings, I thought of myself as the conductor, calling out, "All aboard!" But the response was far less enthusiastic than it had been at the train station. I began to ask myself, Will people get on board? Does everybody *need* to get on board? How will I know if they are on board? The more meetings and conversations we had, the clearer it became that some people would definitely get on board, some never would, and some weren't sure.

I gave names to the three groups: transformers, lost souls, and fence sitters.

Transformers. The transformers had been waiting for a conductor to call "All Aboard!" for a long time. When I met with them, they were aggressive and even angry with the company and its situation. They wanted change immediately, faster than we could make it. They had seen the same things I had seen in the mirror. They were frustrated that they had been unable to make the changes they thought were necessary. They felt suffocated by the organization.

Although I sympathized with them, I did not really understand their feelings of suffocation. What was preventing them from effecting change? What was getting in their way? It wasn't until much later that I realized that the organization itself was largely responsible for their frustration. As a result, the members of this group looked at me with hope that what I was saying about change was real and also with skepticism that anything would ever really happen.

In one meeting, a transformer asked me a very telling question. "Vineet," he said, "thanks for coming here and listening to us. But will we ever see you again?"

That one struck me hard, especially since five hundred people were in the room and listening carefully to my response. I honestly didn't know when or if I would see that group again, but I hadn't quite reached a point where I could be as transparent in my responses as I eventually became. I don't remember exactly what my reply was, but the transformers told me it was unconvincing.

Lost souls. The second set of people are the ones I call lost souls. They would sit in the meetings with frowns on their faces. Whatever we were doing or whatever we proposed to do was, in their opinion, hopeless and wrong. Their negativity went beyond their views on specific plans.

They were convinced that there was absolutely nothing we could do, no plan we could follow, that would ever change anything.

That view might have been tolerable if they had kept it to themselves. But lost souls tend to be vocal in their comments and expressive in their attitudes, and they defuse the energy in any meeting they attend or team they join. If I said something like, "I don't know how we're going to do this, but, trust me, we will get there," the lost souls would pounce on my words. To them, admitting that I didn't know something showed that I was incompetent. They did not see it as honesty or transparency.

Even though I call them lost souls, I do not believe that these people were intentionally obstructionist, that they meant to cause harm, or that they could never make a contribution. They may not even have realized that they came across as negative. I think they often saw themselves as realists and truth tellers, the only ones who really understood how things worked, or didn't.

Fence sitters. The third group of employees, the largest of the three, I call the fence sitters. These people spoke up the least in meetings and rarely asked questions, but they watched the transformers and the lost souls carefully. When our eyes met, they always smiled at me. They said nice things about HCLT when it was expected. But they clearly were in "watch and wait" mode.

After I had classified these three groups, I thought about how to get as many of them on board as possible.

At the time, I had not read Malcolm Gladwell's book *The Tipping Point* with its analysis of how people act as "connectors" and salespeople to bring social movements to an unstoppable point of change. But I was aware of the importance of getting a critical mass of people involved in a change effort and knew that as little as 10 percent of the total company population could be enough, as long as they were the right people.

So I decided to focus on the transformers. If I could get them on board, they would bring along a lot of fence sitters. And as more people boarded the train, the lost souls would either fall silent, leave the company, or perhaps even climb the steps themselves.

I found out, however, that as much as transformers want change, they are smart, observant, and not easily fooled. They listen closely to words but believe that proof is in action. So, as we'll see, it takes much more than a passionate call of "All aboard!" and a promise of a bright future to win them over and get their support and engagement.

Another External Factor: The Excuse Culture

As these conversations were going on, I began to realize that there was another factor involved in the company's current situation and people's attitudes toward it. This factor had to do with the environment outside the company, but not so much with the specific IT landscape as the worldwide business scene. I call it the *excuse culture.*

I began thinking about this in reaction to a curious pattern of behavior I saw in some of our managers. They would look in the mirror, see the truth of the company's situation, and yet feel no obligation to do anything about it. They had become complacent and comfortable with their reality and believed that everything and anything that was wrong was the fault of circumstances beyond their control. They had an excuse for everything:

"The economy is terrible, so nothing can be done."

"Leaders of huge corporations are going to jail for outrageous transgressions, so why should anybody else have to perform up to a high standard?"

"Whole companies are failing and banks are exploding, so we should be happy just to still be in business."

This reasoning drove me a bit crazy, but it made me realize even more the importance of the Mirror Mirror exercise and getting people to see reality as completely as possible. Only then could we begin to get beyond the excuses.

My Own Experience with the Mirror

Let me add here that it is not only employees who must look into the mirror, and not only employees who are good at blaming external factors for their own lack of performance. Leaders are just as likely to avoid the mirror and make all kinds of excuses for themselves.

Fortunately, I had some practice in facing up to reality on a personal level. My first experience with the mirror came soon after I joined HCL as a senior management trainee in 1985. I had just gotten my MBA from XLRI School of Business and Human Resources. I had wanted to join a small company so I could have an impact on its results sooner than I would in a larger organization and, with lots of ideas on how to improve HCL and help it grow, I felt supreme confidence that I would quickly rise up through the ranks. After only three weeks of training, however, I was approached by a senior executive who took me aside and told me that I probably did not have a future with HCL. I was shocked. "Why?" I asked. "Because you haven't paid enough attention to our products," he said. "You care only about strategy."

I couldn't believe my ears. I floundered for something to say and finally turned red and said nothing.

"Look, Vineet," the executive said. "Our business is about products. Unless you master them, you will not get very far at HCL. In fact, you won't get beyond next week."

I went home and spent the evening pacing my room, frustrated and angry, thinking about what I should do. I felt that the executive had a very narrow view of business and I was convinced he was all wrong about me.

Just before I went to bed, however, I looked at myself in the mirror. I did not see the world-beating MBA, the future top executive I imagined myself to be. Instead, I saw a young trainee who, in truth, had not spent enough time learning about the fine points of the company's products and services and how they were different from those of our competitors. I conceded that the executive had a point. I realized that I could not work in a technology company and expect to become a senior executive without a complete understanding of the company's offerings. I had not been seeing reality very clearly.

The image snapped me out of it. I decided to view the experience as an opportunity. I promised myself that I would change my outlook. I went back to training the next day and worked hard at learning the company's products and services, and a month later I was assigned to the role of business manager in the Mumbai office, one of the company's toughest assignments.

That was my first experience with looking in the mirror, recognizing the truth, and deciding that a change was needed. Now, it was necessary for me to do it again. I had to look into the mirror and honestly see myself and the company I was supposed to run.

Looking into the Mirror and Seeing the Past

When I saw our employees looking into the mirror, a strange thing happened. I found that many of them were actually staring into the past, as if they were looking into a rearview mirror at the landscape we had already traveled through.

At first, I didn't understand.

I had been with Comnet for twelve years, after all, and I had become very used to its high-speed, entrepreneurial environment. A start-up, by its very nature, is about the desire to change something: a technology, a company, the world. When we looked in the mirror at Comnet, we caught a glimpse of the future.

So it took me a while to realize that far too many people at HCLT were focused on the past. They were seeing twenty-seven years of achievement. Exciting leaps of growth. National recognition and pride. No wonder the company was steeped in nostalgia for the landscape of yesterday. That may have been the only view that provided much pleasure and comfort. The present was too frustrating. The future was too unknown.

Isn't this true of many companies today? Perhaps your own?

We at HCLT had to stop looking into the past.

But how would I stop it? Should I be brutal and yank away the mirror? Should I say, "You look in the mirror and think that HCLT is still the leader. But, in reality, HCLT is no longer the front-runner it once was"?

No. That would simply be behaving like a traditional, authoritarian CEO. Besides, that approach would only depress people, hurt them, shock them into inaction rather than action.

I had to strike a delicate balance. On the one hand, people had to see that HCLT was no longer the leader it had once been. On the other hand, I did not want to damage the great pride that employees felt in the company and its past glories, as pride can be a great source of strength when coupled with a desire to change.

The only solution I could think of was to create a vision that our people could look forward to, an image much more attractive than what they saw when looking backward, and so appealing they would get excited about what was to come.

But what would that image be? What should our future look like?

Surprising Conversations with Customers

During the Mirror Mirror period, in addition to my meetings with employees around the world, I also met and spoke with many customers.

I vividly remember one of these meetings; it was with the CIO of a global corporation. HCLT had just completed a major, time-critical project for the company, which had gone extremely well. I entered the conference room where the HCLT team and the CIO were waiting.

I was expecting to get a big smile and a handshake from him, to accept a pat on the back, and to hear champagne corks popping.

On the contrary, the CIO barely said a brief hello to me and then focused his attention on the HCLT team. "I want to thank all of you for the excellent work you have done on our project," he said. "Not only have you fulfilled our requirements, but you have gone far beyond our expectations. And it has been a joy to work with you." He gave each of them a hug. Then he turned to me. "Vineet," he said, "you have just come on board. You don't know how lucky you are to have such wonderful people working for you." I was surprised and touched by the emotion in his voice.

The scene made a lasting impression on me.

Not long after that, I attended a very different meeting with a customer. This time, the project had been a disaster. We had failed to execute on time, and we had not met the project specifications. I walked into the room where the project team was waiting, ready to explain to the customer how we would correct our mistakes.

Before I could say a word, he looked me in the eye. "Vineet, your people did everything they could," he said. "The problem was that your organization didn't support them properly. If it had, I'm sure they would have been able to meet our objectives." He was angry at me, not at the team.

Again, I was surprised and struck by the comment.

Neither customer had said a word about our services or products. They had talked only about the team members, the employees they had worked with. Could it be that they saw more value in the individual employees who delivered the services than they did in the services and supporting technologies themselves?

Gen Y

The review of the IT landscape, along with the conversations with employees and customers, made me look more closely at the employees who were creating the most value for our customers. I saw that one group in particular behaved differently from the rest and was most likely to be made up of transformers: the Gen Y employees.

Unlike the longer-serving employees who had become used to the traditional organization, these younger people weren't impressed that I was president. They didn't care so much about titles and positions; they didn't look upward for direction. They asked pointed questions of me. But they didn't expect perfect answers, or any solution at all. They believed in collaboration. They loved to learn. They shared everything—information, music, ideas, feelings. They spent many hours (not all on work time, I hope) on Orkut, Facebook, MySpace, and YouTube, and a lot of them wrote their own blogs to share their ideas with the world.

These people had been the key members of the teams that my conversations with customers had been about. They were the ones who did the real work. The ones who met with customers. Who delivered our products and services. Who worked through problems. Who deserved support and praise.

I realized that they themselves were the value we offered customers. Taken together, they created the value zone within the company's organization. Without them, without that zone of value, HCLT was nothing but a shell, layers and layers of management or aggregators with controls and processes that had nothing to offer to the customers.

That was why that first customer had hugged every one of the team members, but not me. And why the second customer had blamed me, not the team, for the company's failure. They saw that management did not live in the value zone or anywhere near it. They recognized that, in fact, management at times got in the way of creating value. Management did not say to the employees in the value zone, "What can we do to help you?" Instead, we wasted their precious time and energy by requiring them to make endless presentations to us about irrelevant things and write reports about what they had or had not done.

Not only did we have to stop wasting their time, but we also had to find a way to put the value zone at the center of the organization.

The Age-Old Pyramid

These observations made me realize that we needed to hold up the mirror to the organization itself, not just to the employees. What was the reality of the HCLT organizational structure?

It did not take a great deal of effort to determine that it was a traditional hierarchy—the age-old pyramid, with the few on the top, most on the bottom, and the many in between. The value zone, the place where the essential work of the company was accomplished, had long been considered the R&D and manufacturing departments, where products were created and produced. That's where the faster chips had been developed, new technologies devised, and smarter features added.

But as my conversations with customers and my observations of the GenY transformers proved, the new knowledge economy had changed all that. The value zone no longer lay in the technology itself and certainly not in any specific piece of hardware or software. Customers could choose among many technologies, from a variety of suppliers, all of which would probably enable them to achieve their goals.

The value zone now lay in the way the technologies were brought together and implemented—the *how* of our offering, more than the what. But those people were not properly respected or supported within the archaic pyramid that had been designed to exalt those with hierarchical power rather than those who created customer value.

Serving the Value Zone

I mulled over this problem. How could we strengthen the value zone? How could we move the focus away from the *what* of our offering to the *how* of delivering value? What could management do differently?

A radical image came into my mind: an inverted pyramid. What if we could turn the traditional organization upside down? What if management was accountable to the value zone and the people in it, not just the other way around? What if the organizational pyramid could be *inverted*? The bottom would become the top, the top would be at the bottom.

Employees first.

Customers second.

Management . . . third?

If we could do that, wouldn't we have something very powerful? Wouldn't it enable us to transform the way we deliver value to our customers and make the zone between our customers and our employees into something special?

After all, not every company can create an innovative new product or service; not every company can be a Google or a Facebook. We have to find other ways to differentiate ourselves, to create real and distinct value for our customers. But wouldn't this kind of transformation set us apart from our competitors and help us throw off the baggage of long ago? Wouldn't it help us become more engaged with our employees and fire their imaginations? Wouldn't such a transformation, made from the ground up, be more sustainable? Was this the way to build the competitive advantage we so desperately needed?

I knew the answer was yes.

Aspiring to Point B:
The Romance of Tomorrow

The inverted pyramid was the germ of the idea that eventually, after much discussion with my management team and people throughout the company, was expressed in the phrase Employees First, Customers Second (EFCS).

It is one thing, however, for a leader to have an idea and quite another thing for an organization to embrace it. I knew it would not be enough for me to make speeches to our employees about organizational structures, value zones, competitive differentiators, and EFCS. I had to make everyone see the future image of point B that would replace the image of the past that they liked so much.

And it had to be attractive. When a teenage girl or boy looks in the mirror, what does he or she see? Barack Obama. Oprah Winfrey. Steve Jobs. Or A. R. Rahman, the composer who won two Oscars for *Slumdog Millionaire?*

The teenagers fall into the romance of tomorrow, into the aspiration of point B. I wanted our employees to be like teenagers again, with visions of endless possibilities ahead.

So, all that spring, I spent hundreds of hours talking to people throughout the company, exploring this idea of the inverted pyramid and how it related to the idea of Employees First, Customers Second. I wanted them to understand that we needed to shake things up, put management in service to the employees in the value zone, and bring more of the characteristics of Gen Y into the workplace. I also wanted them to know that change did not mean we would devalue the good things that HCLT had accomplished over the years or the great people we had in the workforce.

I used stories and metaphors to help get my meaning across, as I continue to do, and as I do throughout this book. "Think about the diamond cutter," I said. "He starts with a rough stone and uses his skills to make it beautiful. Or think of the potter. She takes raw clay and shapes it into a wonderful vase. If there were no imperfections in the world, we would not need the diamond cutter or the potter. The same is true of business. Would you rather work in a company where everything was perfect and nothing needed to be changed? Or would you rather be in a company that needs to be transformed?"

Just as with our discussions of point A, as we discussed point B we found that groups fell into the now-expected categories: transformers, lost souls, and fence sitters.

Although the stories and metaphors fired up our transformers, it seemed that there would never be enough of them to reach a tipping point. As time went along, however, and as people asked better and more pointed questions and as our conversations grew deeper and increasingly genuine, more and more employees began to get excited about the image of the inverted pyramid. They understood that the reason the company was going to be a better place to work was that management was depending on them to bring about a change. Not only did more and more people within the company climb on board, many of the frustrated transformers who had left the company started to return.

Walking the Roads of Three Heroes

As we went about this process at HCLT, I thought about my three heroes—Mahatma Gandhi, Nelson Mandela, and Martin Luther King Jr.—and how they had created transformation in their societies. I realized that although they had made many speeches and taken many stands, these three leaders were known for far more than their specific actions. They had also transformed the mind-set of their people, and the new way of thinking had lasted long beyond their lifetimes.

These great leaders did not formulate strategy by retreating with their top people to a private place and then emerging to make a pronouncement to the masses. No, they walked the roads of their countries, met their people, and talked with them ceaselessly. During that process, they held up the mirror to their societies and helped their people see and articulate what was wrong. The leaders were able to make people intrinsically unhappy with the current state of affairs without demeaning their accomplishments or dishonoring their past in any way. Gandhi, Mandela, and King helped their countrymen to see point A. They also worked with their people to create an idea of the future, the point B that made people aspire to change. The resulting combination of dissatisfaction, continued pride, and excitement was a very, very heady potion and difficult to reject.

I do not claim, of course, that we at HCLT were the only ones who followed this transformation path. Many other companies created their own versions of our Mirror Mirror exercise and developed their own processes for identifying points A and B.

Moreover, although this book is focused on how we used the Mirror Mirror exercise to start our own transformation in 2005, we relied on it again during the worldwide economic troubles of 2008. We held up the mirror to ourselves then to see where we were and how we were reacting to the situation. In other words, the Mirror Mirror process is just one element in a continuous cycle. It helped us change in 2005. We brought out the mirror again in 2007 so that we could clearly see the progress we had made and celebrate it. We looked into it again in 2008, when the challenges facing the company had changed. It is important to understand that the Mirror Mirror concept happens periodically throughout a company's life, not just once.

I didn't completely understand where we were headed in those spring days of 2005. I saw that people had looked in the mirror and that many were seeing the reality of our point A. This had created the necessary aspiration for change. I also believed that the Employees First, Customers Second concept was beginning to catch on. But, now that we had gotten the company to understand the present and look toward the possibilities of the future, I saw that there was no path connecting the two dots. I realized that we had taken only the very first step in our journey of transformation.

The truly hard part lay ahead.

CHAPTER TWO

Trust Through Transparency

Creating a Culture of Change

Summer descended. One steamy afternoon, I sat in my office and asked myself, What do we do next?

The Mirror Mirror exercise had served its function: to help us see the reality of our situation, to create dissatisfaction with the status quo, and to build a hunger for change in the company. The anxiety and concern that some had expressed during that period had largely been replaced by a new energy and excitement. People felt good to be talking about movement and growth and how we could be a great company again.

Beneath the excitement, however, there was still plenty of skepticism and uncertainty.

The idea of Employees First, Customers Second sounded promising—if you're an employee, why wouldn't it seem positive?—but what exactly did it mean? *How* would we put employees first, and why would we put customers second? Did it mean that we would increase salaries and have pizza parties on Fridays? Did it mean we would actually change our organizational structure? Did it mean we no longer had to work within the budgets and meet the schedules our customers set? Were we truly serious about this concept of focusing so sharply on the employees in the value zone? Or was it just superficial talk, intended to make people feel good? Or, worse, was it really just a prelude to downsizing?

People started debating the future vision of HCLT and I saw this as a good sign. It had been a long time since employees were interested enough in where we were headed to discuss it during meetings and over lunch, a long time since they felt that what they had to say would be listened to and would make a difference in how the company operated. That was a change in itself, but hardly the transformation we were looking for. As our next move, we had to figure out exactly where to go, strategically, and how to get there, practically.

These goals can seem very difficult when you're in the middle of figuring out how to achieve them. There are so many levers to pull, so many people to influence, so many courses of action that could be taken. I obviously did not have all the answers myself. I didn't even know all the questions to ask. Nor was I familiar with the specific issues in every one of our businesses or country operations. I decided it was time to call a meeting of my hundred most senior managers to discuss with them our future and how to get there.

The *Blueprint* Meeting

In early July 2005, my A team, the hundred best and brightest brains in the company, flew in to Delhi from around the world for a three-day conference. Many of us had met in various smaller groups before, but this was the first meeting in which we all came together to focus on the specific question: What should we do next together?

Next. Together. Those were the fundamental words. Could we come up with the answer to the question "What do we do next, together?" We called the meeting Blueprint, and our goal was to draw a path from point A to point B.

On the first day, I had planned to present my initial ideas for our strategy. These had emerged from a lot of work with a group of very smart members of my strategic marketing team. We had considered many strategic options and narrowed them down to two. One of the ideas—to compete against the global players for much larger customer engagements—looked very bold, perhaps too bold for us to pull off, but offered the largest and most significant opportunity for HCLT. The other was more conventional and less daring and probably represented only an incremental improvement. Both had their advantages, and I was of two minds about them, as were many members of my marketing group—so much so that we had prepared two versions of my remarks, one for the bold strategy, and one for the more modest approach. I had stayed up late the night before, thinking them over. At last I went to sleep, still uncertain which road to go.

I woke around 5 A.M. and reached for my cell phone. I read a text message from one of the team members: "Vineet. Go for the big idea. We are all with you."

The message struck me as encouraging, but also odd. Did it mean they would *not* be with me if I went with plan B? I realized that the big ideas are the ones that attract the most talented people and bring out the best in them. My colleagues were telling me that they wanted to go for the big move, the impossible.

I thought back to a decision of similar magnitude that I had made in 1993: to found Comnet on the idea of remote network management. We thought the idea was very compelling and had huge potential, but it also carried a lot of risk. We decided to go for it and the result was completely worth the effort. Remembering that past decision helped me make up my mind about the current one. I shot a message back to the team: "Let's go for the bold one!"

But what about the hundred best and brightest that I had invited to this meeting? Would they support the plan the marketing team and I had drawn? I had a nervous sensation in my stomach as I dressed. The last thing I wanted to do was get excited, reach too far, and fall flat. But we would never know the answer unless we presented the question.

My marketing team and I got to the conference room early. We thought that if we arrived before everyone else, we would improve our chances of success. Soon enough, the hundred started rolling in. We shook hands, hugged some old friends. Everyone was smiling. People said nice things. But my stomach was still churning.

At last everyone was seated. The lights dimmed a bit. I walked to the podium. One of the communications strategies that has worked well for me is to start by plunging right in to the main idea. If you identify the elephant in the room in the first few minutes, you put yourself on the path toward success or disaster—a path that is pretty much irreversible.

"Let me share five interesting facts with you," I began. "Fact number one: the worldwide IT outsourcing market is worth about $500 billion. The industry is dominated by the global players like IBM, Accenture, and EDS. Fact two: the top five Indian IT companies, including HCL, account for just $6 billion of that total. That is just 1 percent."

I paused for a moment. I wanted everyone to focus on just how enormous our market was, how tiny a share of it we actually had, and what a narrow segment we played in.

"Fact three: the Indian IT players seem to have become satisfied with this 1 percent. They have gotten used to a business model that is narrowly focused and can be easily scaled. Competitive advantage comes from hiring and training young, college-educated engineers and deploying them to deliver high-quality services."

I paused again. Everyone knew that this was the truth of our industry and that we had been depending on an endless supply of talent to build scale for years.

"Fact four: IT outsourcing customers are seeking higher transparency, greater flexibility, and more attention from their global IT players, and they are increasingly frustrated with these suppliers because they don't always deliver. Fact five: the total-outsourcing model that was dominant in the 1990s, largely led by the Big Four, in which clients got locked into ten-year deals and lost control of their IT, is not working for customers anymore. They want to regain some control by collaborating with their outsourcers rather than leaving everything to them."

With the facts laid out, it was time to move on to the proposed solution. "We know that of the G-1,000, the thousand major global companies, the top two hundred are quite well served," I said. "The G-200 are the customers that everyone is chasing, and the Big Four catch them most often. So why don't we focus on the next eight hundred, the ones that are not so well taken care of? There is no reason we can't integrate our services so we can manage the complete IT life cycle for our customers and take on the role of partner rather than supplier. These types of contracts can run into the hundreds of millions of dollars."

This was, indeed, a bold idea. It caused some fidgeting in the audience. At that time, HCLT offered discrete IT services, which generally meant smaller contracts. Most of our relationships with customers were not the kinds of strategic partnerships that the global players had with their clients.

There was a nervous cough or two. People shifted in their seats. I glanced at my team, saw a nod or two of encouragement, and plunged ahead.

"Now, how will we go about winning this business? How will we get companies to think differently about HCLT? By offering a real strategic difference based on three fundamental beliefs. First, we will offer flexibility and transparency of a kind customers have never seen before, not from us, or from our new direct competitors, the big global players. Second, we will sharply focus on value centricity. By that, I mean we will put all our energy into increasing the value we are creating for our customers rather than trying to build the volume of business we do with them. Third, and most important, we will set a new standard for the value we actually deliver. And that is where Employees First, Customers Second comes in. It is what will enable us to unleash the positive energy and passion of our employees, to create a tremendous *wow!* in the value zone that will become our major differentiator."

I paused and let this sink in for a moment.

"This cannot happen overnight, of course," I continued. "To transform HCLT from a provider of discrete outsourced services to a strategic IT services partner, from a developer of technology to an investor in core intellectual property, will take five years. It will require a reorganization of the company structure, from a collection of business units to a matrix organization that can integrate services and do it worldwide." And I knew it would take much more, as I went on to describe. "We will have to rejuvenate those employees who have lost their enthusiasm, improve outdated processes, build strategic partnerships, and develop new products and services." I concluded, "We must not waste our time and energy pursuing small, easy-to-win, nonstrategic opportunities, but we cannot fail to grow in any year, either. In short, we have a hell of a lot of work to do."

I turned over the last page of my notes. I looked out at the audience and asked for the lights to be brought up a little. The hundred members of our A team had listened attentively, but I did not see a lot of expression on their faces.

"Now, I would like to hear from you," I said. "Does the strategy make sense? What are your thoughts?" I looked at the young colleagues on my team. They seemed to be collectively holding their breath.

I waited. Silence. Nothing. Thirty seconds passed. A minute. I swear that two full minutes went by, and still no one said a word. This was unprecedented. I could not remember another time when members of this group had been so reluctant to speak their minds. At last, one of the business leaders from Europe, whom I will call Alex, raised his hand.

"Yes, Alex," I said. "What are you thinking?"

"Vineet," he said, "I'm thinking that you must be crazy."

"Possibly," I said. "Why do you think so?"

"We have never done anything like this before," he said. "We have no idea how to compete with the global players. We will destroy everything we have created in the past few years. Instead of going after these big contracts, we should first get better at executing on our current business model."

I said nothing. I did not want to get involved in defending my ideas. I wanted debate. Another manager spoke up.

"I agree with Alex," she said. "Taking a big leap is all very well, but we can't abandon our core competence. That is a recipe for disaster."

The temperature in the room was rising. People began shifting in their seats and whispering to one another. A business leader from the United States stood up. "I agree with Vineet," he said. "Our current business model is out-dated. Our employees know it. Our customers know it. Our competitors know it. Haven't we already faced up to the reality of where we are? Don't we see customers leaving us every day? Our shareholders asking tough questions about our future? Talented people walking out our doors and going to work for our competitors? We are already good at our current business model. But it no longer works!"

Another voice chimed in: "We have been in this industry for over two decades and have been number one for many of those years—but not once in the last five years. Now, we're not even in the top three. We have to take a bold step!" More voices rose from around the room, and soon a heated discussion was taking place. I stepped back. I wanted the A team to talk, not me. In truth, it didn't really matter what they said about the global services strategy. What mattered is that they started talking truth, rather than going on about the normal, fine-sounding plans and programs that would keep driving us into the ground. These were the hundred brightest people in the company. If they decided to kill the plan I had presented, I was confident they would come up with something equally big and probably better. We needed a big change, but it did not have to be the one I had proposed.

So the discussion continued. I wanted all the comments to come out into the open and be debated to the point of exhaustion.

The Trust Quotient

The strategy discussion at the Blueprint meeting went on for the better part of that first day. I listened and watched

as, over the course of the afternoon, three distinct positions emerged.

The transformers loved the idea of change and would
hear no objections to it. Their enthusiasm was exciting
and infectious, if not yet completely grounded in reality
and practicality.

The fence sitters believed that something new needed
to be done, but they had questions and concerns about
the global IT services strategy, and some of these people
suggested other strategies we might pursue. They kept
asking questions, adding information, and working to
make up their minds.

We did not have any lost souls, those negative thinkers
of the larger HCLT population, among the hundred
brightest minds of the A team. But we did have a third
group composed of what I call the "yes, but" managers. For
every idea or proposal, these managers had an objection.
"That's all very well," they would say, "but . . ." And the
"but" was always about why this idea could never work or
how that idea had already been tried or how this solution
would cost too much or could never be executed. I had
heard the "yes, buts" many times throughout my career. I
had seen how these objections could stop an organization
from facing the naked truth. In this case, the "yes, but"
managers viewed the proposed strategy as too big a risk, for
themselves and for the company. For every new proposal,
they found new reasons why the plan couldn't work, and
many of their reservations were completely plausible.

But as the afternoon turned into evening, the trans-formers tempered their enthusiasm with a dose of reality. The fence sitters, one by one, made up their minds. And the "yes, buts" gradually had their objections met or dismissed. At last, the top hundred reached a consensus that we needed to make a bold move, that provision of integrated services made sense, and that the principles of transparency, flexibility, value centricity, and the EFCS approach could create a powerful differentiator for HCLT.

I was impressed by the quality of the conversation and by the engagement of the management team. I had entered the meeting wondering whether we had the people we needed on board. Now I felt certain that with only a couple of question marks, we did.

When we came to the end of the day, I stepped to the podium to close the session. "I want to thank you for this conversation," I said. "For expressing everything that is in your minds and in your hearts. Now that we have come to a general agreement on our strategy, we come to the most difficult part of all—execution and change management. And that will be our discussion for tomorrow."

I paused and looked out over the audience. I was startled, even troubled, by what I saw. In an instant, the looks in the managers' eyes had changed. A moment before, they had looked weary, but satisfied, confident that we had aired our differences, engaged in a real conversation, and come out on the other side. Why did many of them now look so uncertain? Why, when I looked from face to face, did some of them avert their gaze? What had I said?

And then I understood the problem. I had spoken the words "execution" and "change." Those two words had provoked the different look in their eyes. I saw that many members of my senior team did not truly trust that they could execute on the strategy and manage the complex organizational change. They did not trust that I could execute on the strategy, that their employees could execute, or that the entire company could pull it off.

I was confronting the difference between being convinced by an idea and trusting that it can be executed. We have all seen great orators speak and win over crowds at enormous gatherings. The orator describes in stirring tones a great vision, a whole new way forward. The crowd cheers and shouts in approval. Then they go home and think, "That was a great speech, but what that person said will never happen."

I wanted to be sure that I was not fooling myself. All eyes were on me, and I could see that although a few of the managers were confident that we could take on the challenge ahead, not enough of them were.

"Well, Vineet," I said to myself in that moment, "it's not going to work. Without trust from the management team, the game will be over before it begins."

In hindsight, I wonder why I thought they would trust me at all. What we were proposing was pretty radical. Why *should* they trust me? Just because I was asking them to?

No. That is not a reason to trust anyone, especially in today's world. Employees have distrusted managers since there have been employees and managers, but I was sure the distrust that ran within the organization was deeper than ever before. Over the past decade, we have seen many business executives and managers who have lied and stolen and betrayed the trust of their people and their companies. The distrust of people in positions of authority and power extends into every walk of life. The *trust quotient,* therefore, particularly regarding business leadership, is at an all-time low around the world. If you are a CEO or senior executive, you must not allow yourself to imagine that you, as a leader, or your company, no matter how successful, is immune to this problem. It is natural for a CEO or senior executive to think, "I am nothing like the ones who were tossed out of their companies or ended up in jail. My people know me. They know that I am a trustworthy person."

I suggest that you think again. If your organization has more than a couple of hundred people in it, most of them don't know you. You know you are trustworthy, but they do not. I believe that your personal trust quotient is lower than you think it is—probably quite a bit lower.

If I had any illusions about my trust quotient before the Blueprint meeting, I had none at the end of that first day's discussion. Please do not misunderstand what I am saying. I did not see *distrust* in my managers' eyes. I just did not see complete, 100 percent trust. Not being distrusted, however, is not good enough to embark on an important transformation.

I also realized that the lack of trust was not confined to me. The people in the room did not trust each other 100 percent. From what I read into their dubious looks, it was clear that they did not have complete faith that their colleagues could pull off what we had decided. And if they couldn't have faith in their own people, the distrust was probably mutual.

So, what should have been obvious even before the Blueprint meeting began, now became blindingly clear: before we did anything, we would have to find a way to build trust throughout the organization. Not trust in me, as their leader, only. Not trust in a particular strategy. But trust in each other.

Lack of trust, we had discovered, was the most important "yes, but" of all.

The Nature of Trust

I have thought a lot about trust over the years, as I have worked with people who say, "I want you to trust me." Or, "We must build a trust relationship." These statements puzzle me. What are they actually proposing? I have also done a great deal of reading about trust. David Maister, for example, writes about the management of professional service firms, where trust between consultants and clients is extremely important and quite personal. One of the books he coauthored is *The Trusted Advisor*. Maister says there are four dimensions of trust:

Credibility: Credibility comes from professional expertise. If the person possesses deep knowledge and follows good practice, you feel trust in what he or she says and does.

Did I have credibility at the time of the Blueprint meeting? Perhaps. Certainly I was credible when I talked about the state of our business. But how could anyone know whether I could be trusted in what I was saying about long-term strategy?

Reliability: Reliability is revealed through actions over time. If you have observed a person's activities and respect them, you probably trust that the person will do what he or she says, the person is dependable and will behave in certain ways.

Did my managers think of me as reliable in July of 2005? Probably they didn't think of me as reliable or unreliable, because they didn't have enough experience to tick the box either way.

Intimacy: This aspect of trust is about emotions. You instinctively feel that you can or cannot discuss many kinds of issues with a certain person.

During the Mirror Mirror exercise in the months before the Blueprint meeting, I had hundreds of conversations with employees throughout HCLT, individually and in meetings big and small. It was an emotional experience for everyone, including me. But my people had not seen the result of this emotion sharing and soul searching. I might yet betray them.

Self-orientation: The self-oriented dimension is Maister's fourth aspect of trust. This one, though, *reduces* the trust quotient. It is about your motives and the things you care about. Can I trust you to think beyond your own self-interest?

What did my managers think about my motives? Did I just want to increase my own personal power? Did I want to appoint my friends to important positions? Did I wish to get lots of media exposure? It was hard to see how the Employees First idea would exalt the CEO, but people make all kinds of assumptions about a leader's motives.

If I think about my trust quotient at the time of the Blueprint meeting and evaluate it on Maister's four elements of trust—credibility, reliability, intimacy, and self-orientation—I am not surprised that I saw a lack of trust in the eyes of my hundred senior managers. In that moment, I realized that our first job would be to build trust throughout the organization.

The Family Model

We know about the importance of building trust from the family units we live in. All my life, I have been a student of the institution of family, which I view as a micro-organization that holds many lessons for large companies.

Many of my thoughts about management spring from observing my own family: my parents and grandparents, my wife and me, and our two children. We are fortunate to have built a great deal of trust into our relationships, and I believe that we have a strong and trusting family. So, as I thought about creating trust at HCLT, I naturally looked towards family units for insight.

Throughout my career, I have been puzzled by the way that businesspeople separate themselves into two parts. Each morning, we say good-bye to our families, come to work, hang our coats on a hook, and in that comfortable coat we wore from home, we leave behind all our emotions, subjectivity, personality, and connections to family life. We don our stiff white collars and put our heads down and go to work. We abide by the systems and practices and unwritten rules of the workplace:

Do not trust your manager.

Don't get too emotional about anything.

Remember, it's not personal; it's only business.

These are outdated thoughts left over from the early years of the industrial age, when jobs were largely mechanical and business organizations felt they had to protect themselves through command-and-control methods.

Families used to operate this way, too. In the traditional family, parents were the ultimate authorities. The children were expected to follow the rules and do as they were told. If they did not, they were punished.

In the past several decades, however, the family unit has changed considerably. Parents wish to be friends and mentors and advisers to their children. The kids want to be trusted to live quite independently.

The best families are those that have a culture of trust. The parents trust their children to come to them with problems. The children trust their parents to support and protect them, but also to let them have their freedom. I recall the old story about a child who will jump from the roof of the family home into the outstretched arms of the father waiting below, even if the child is blind.

But if trust does not exist in a family, the parents may battle with the children and with each other. The kids get in trouble or leave home. The parents have their own problems, personally or at work. The family becomes dysfunctional or breaks apart, just as high-performing companies can lose momentum in the absence of a trusting environment. But, I asked myself, how does one go about building, in a company, the kind of trust that exists in strong families?

The Elements of Transparency

On the second day of the Blueprint conference, I talked with my A team, my hundred brightest managers, about the importance of trust at HCLT.

Could transparency really be the catalyst to drive trust? I believed so, for several good reasons. Before I describe them, however, it's necessary to understand a bit about the culture at HCLT. I compared it often to Comnet, where the culture was much easier to see and understand. It was largely driven by product and service innovation. We believed that if we did not innovate every eighteen months or so, if we did not bring a new product or a new service to the market, we would not remain competitive and would lose our position as a leader. We saw regular transformation as an essential part of our culture, driven by the nature of the business we were in.

Obviously, this was not the case at HCLT, a legacy business that had grown rapidly and changed quickly in its early years. As it grew bigger, it gradually slowed down. Change became more difficult and took longer to implement. Too many bright ideas got left on the table.

But I saw that the culture at HCLT was not all about legacy. We had bright people and strong leaders who wanted to break free of the old ways. We saw this very clearly in the Mirror Mirror exercise and again in the Blueprint meeting. As is true in so many large companies,

it was the HCLT organization—the archaic pyramid—
that was shackling people and keeping them from contributing all they could and in the ways they longed to.

I believed that one of the ways we could release this talent was to make our culture participative. To get our people to participate more, we had to create a culture of trust
and to do that we needed much more transparency. There
are five main ways in which transparency builds trust.

First, transparency ensures that every stakeholder knows
the company's vision and understands exactly how his or
her contribution assists the organization in achieving its
goals. Working in an environment without transparency
is like trying to solve a jigsaw puzzle without knowing
what the finished picture is supposed to look like.

Second, transparency helps to ensure that every stakeholder has a deep, personal commitment to the aims of
the organization.

Third, for the Gen Y members of our workforce
transparency is a given. They post their life stories in public domains; they expect nothing less in their workplaces.

Fourth, in a knowledge economy, we want customers to
be transparent with us, to share their ideas, their visions for
the future, and their strategies for solving core problems.
Without such transparency, how can we create the technology solutions that will accelerate their growth and strength-
en their businesses? And why would a customer be transparent with a potential partner like us if that company does
not trust its employees enough to be transparent with them?

Finally, knowledge companies like HCLT often do lateral hires—people brought in from outside the company—to work on specific projects or initiatives. The only way these outsiders can get up to speed quickly and be as effective as possible is through sharing of information and complete transparency about the strengths and weaknesses, the issues and concerns, of the assignment. The more transparent the process, the more trust that the outsiders felt in the organization, the more we could reduce the amount of learning time, which would give us an advantage over our competitors.

The Amsterdam Window

I remember a visit I once made to a friend's home in Amsterdam. Its huge windows faced one of the city's main canals. The home was flooded with light, and the rooms felt very exposed to the glances of people on the street and in boats on the canal. My friend's home was typical of all the houses in the central part of Amsterdam.

"Why do you have such large windows?" I asked my friend. A stupid question, perhaps, but—after he mentioned all the obvious reasons like letting in light and getting a nice view—I got a much more interesting answer.

"It keeps the house clean," he said.

He didn't explain further, but I took his answer to mean that the bigger your windows, the more glass you

have in your house, the more visible the dirt will be —
to you and to everyone who visits or passes by. If you can
see the dirt, you will be much more likely to get rid of it.

A transparent house, therefore, has a dramatic effect on
the culture inside.

In the house of HCLT, the Mirror Mirror exercise had
been, in a way, about transparency. We had talked openly
and honestly about the issues at the company. But the
activity was limited in scope and duration, and not yet
embedded into the organization or its processes.

At the Blueprint meeting, after we adjourned the formal session on the second day, we reconvened for cocktails
and dinner. Having joined in many conversations during
that long evening, I became increasingly convinced that
we were all more or less on the same page. We had not
ironed out all the details, and we saw a long and difficult
road ahead, but we felt a sense of unity and agreement.

The next day, we came together once more to review
our conclusions and draft a simple blueprint that would
define our future state or point B and articulate in broad
terms the *what* of our offering and, most important, the
how. At last, weary but with a sense of accomplishment,
we dispersed to our different corners of the world. I wondered what the managers would tell their people about
the meeting when they returned to their offices and were
asked, "Did it go well?" Would they say, "Yes, but . . ."? Or
would they say, "We have a great opportunity ahead of us.
Let's get to work."?

I knew that all eyes would be on these hundred managers. Now it was up to them to influence their own top hundred, and so on down the line. That is how we would engage the entire company in our journey of change.

A Novel Approach to Transparency

After the Blueprint meeting, we faced the problem of how, exactly, we would increase the transparency of the organization in order to build trust. How could we let the light in, as the windows did in my friend's house in Amsterdam?

I knew that we must not deal in half measures. We had to do more than crack open a small window of transparency. We had to throw it wide open—do things we had never done before and attempt things that other companies had not tried.

Looking back, the solutions we came up with seem quite obvious. But at the time, I had no easy answers.

I appealed to our bright sparks for ideas and asked my managers to reach out and listen, as well. We got a lot of responses. Many of the ideas, although provocative, were too far out, too difficult to implement. One idea, however, made a great deal of sense.

Opening the Window of Information

The idea was to open the window of financial information.

At the time, our people had access to the financial information that pertained to their own projects, but they had no way of knowing how their business unit and the whole organization were doing. Nor could they compare the performance of their team to that of others in the company. What if we allowed *everybody* to see *all* the business units' and the company's financial data? Wouldn't that be an important step toward greater transparency? Wouldn't it help build a culture of trust—showing that we had nothing to hide and were willing to share both the good and the bad, just as one would in a strong family?

I floated the idea. Immediately came the "yes, buts." There were two major objections.

First, the "yes, buts" asked, wouldn't people get demotivated when they discovered that they were not doing as well as their managers had been telling them? I heard this many times, from many people.

Second came another objection: What would happen if the information leaked out to the press? What if our competition got hold of it? The "yes, buts" worried that all hell would break loose. I saw real fear on this one.

These were fair points, I had to admit. However, I argued, the instant we opened the information window, people would see that some business units were rolling downhill or were underperforming compared with other units. They would also have a true picture of the overall performance of the company. "Our employees told us in Mirror Mirror that they want to climb up," I reminded them. "How can they know how steep the hill is without seeing the road? Are there risks involved? Yes, but it is all part of trusting our employees. Putting their needs first. These are risks we must take."

Once again, I saw cautious agreement, with a skeptical glint in the corner of some eyes.

I turned to our internal IT team. I believed that using our IT system was core to the successful execution of new ideas. I had faith that this team could roll out virtually any bold idea and make it work for employees around the world. I asked the team to create a system that would show the financial performance of each employee's team and be available on his or her desktop.

In just a few weeks, the new system was up and running. The employees loved it immediately. Some of the managers loved it quite a bit less.

When I discovered why, I realized there was a third "yes, but" that no one had articulated to me. Opening the window of information shed a lot of light on the role of the manager. Some found themselves exposed to the glances of the passersby from the streets and canals of the company. People saw that some of the managers were little more than aggregators and brokers of information. These managers' entire authority lay in their control of the information. As soon as everyone had access to it, their power might come into question.

The transformers, however, especially loved the new system. They used the information to instill new energy and direction into their teams. Because all their team members shared the same version of the financial data, they could focus better on what actions to take. With each passing day, the information analysis improved. As people could see the benchmarks and compare their performance with that of others, they worked harder to improve their own performance. Soon, we added nonfinancial information and implemented the balanced scorecard for all our businesses through this process and made it visible for everyone to see on their desktops.

Increased transparency led to quicker action at the grassroots level. It also motivated the teams that were doing well. They felt that their success was being recognized, and they worked even harder to remain in the top-performer club. A new sense of purpose and direction was quite visible in the teams. Now that they had the information they needed, they could spend more time on execution and less time searching for data and trying to understand the reality of their performance.

I should say, however, that the other two "yes, buts" proved to be valid.

Some employees were, indeed, demotivated by the information they saw. And, yes, some information did leak out in ways that caused embarrassment and complication. On balance, however, the positives far outweighed the negatives. When you open the window, you must expect that a fly or two will buzz in to annoy you or that a vase could fall out onto the street and shatter.

However, the effects of the rush of fresh air and brilliant sunlight more than made up for those minor problems.

Opening Up the Office of the CEO: The U&I Portal

Too much happened in those hot summer months of 2005 for me to recount it all, but I want to describe one other way we brought greater transparency to our organization.

As I mentioned earlier, in my early days as president, and then CEO, I spent a lot of time visiting offices around the world and talking with employees at all levels. I heard lots and lots of questions, not all of which I could answer, either because there wasn't enough time to do so or because I simply didn't know the answer. When that happened, I would say, "Shoot me an e-mail. I'll get back to you."

When I said this, many employees did not look satisfied or convinced. They thought I was just dodging the question. They figured they would "shoot me an e-mail" and no answer would ever come back. But I really wanted to answer their questions. At Comnet, we worked in an open office space, and I was used to people calling out questions across the room.

At HCLT, with tens of thousands of employees and offices all over the world, we had to find some way to create the equivalent of the open office. If we did not, the office of the CEO (i.e., the position, and not me personally) would hold too much power. What the office said—or what people *said* it said—would always take precedence over what any employee might say or do.

How could we create the sense of an open office at HCLT?

While I was working with my social networking group, we came up with an idea we called U&I—an online forum where any employee could post any question, which I, along with my leadership team, would answer. The idea was to build an open site where everyone would be able to see the question, the questioner, and the answer. It was a simple idea that we hoped would foster a culture of open conversation, with fewer rumors and less misinformation, and that would thus create more trust. Today, I see forums like this in many companies, but in 2005, I believe it was a breakthrough. Many of these sites, however, are not sufficiently open. They enable people to ask questions directly of the CEO, but neither the questions nor the answers can be seen by others. Such one-on-one dialogues are good but do not create the kind of transparent culture that builds trust.

There were many "yes, buts" to the U&I concept. As with the posting of financial information, two of these doubts stood out.

One: "Some employees will ask really tough questions. They will expose weaknesses that some people don't know about. This could get out of control. It could leak out. We could be in for real trouble."

Two: "Only employees who have problems will ask questions, not the people who see good things or who are satisfied. This will skew the picture. HCLT will look like a much bigger mess than it actually is."

These objections rang true. I talked with many people about them. I consulted my leadership team. I wondered if this initiative might be taking the idea of transparency too far, since all our dirty linen would now be aired in public.

Just when I was about to pull the plug on the idea, I put myself through a personal Mirror Mirror exercise. How could we create trust through transparency if the members of management were the only ones who decided what questions could be asked and answered? Was this not the reason the office of the CEO was such an indomitable power center, because it totally controlled the official conversation? If the CEO was afraid of what would leap out of the cupboard, how could this executive be trusted, and how could management as a whole be trusted? We had to keep pushing open the window. We went for it and launched the site called U&I.

Again, the fears of the doubters were justified. The U&I site was clogged with cribs and complaints, harangues and imprecations that the company was wrong about everything. The comments and questions came pouring in and would not stop. Most of what people said was true. Much of it hurt.

One day, I was speaking to a group of employees, and I expressed my frustration with the questions we were receiving on U&I. I asked what they thought about it, and their answers amazed me.

"This is the biggest change we have seen at HCLT in years," they said. "Now we have a leadership team that is willing to acknowledge the dirt." There was much less gossip now, they said, and fewer rumors flying around the company. People felt that management was listening to their views, and thus there was increased hope that someone, somewhere, would do something about it. Most important, the employees said, they had a leadership team that did not claim to know the answers when it didn't, or say it could fix something when it couldn't. The people said they trusted the leadership team more. They sensed that the team really got it.

One day I received an interesting e-mail that pointed out another aspect of the portal and how people used it.

"You are making a mistake in assuming that U&I is solely about open and honest conversations between the employees and the leadership team," the e-mail read. "Many others around the person who asks the question get involved in the conversation, too. They pounce on that person, offer their own views, and help the commenter see things in a different light. Yes, the response from the leader is important, but a lot of discussion takes place beyond that exchange. Also, it brings issues to the attention of other employees in other parts of the organization who may not have been aware of the problem, and they may start working on the problem since they believe they have the answers."

Another wow! I finally understood the power of what we had created. The U&I site had become a way to transfer the responsibility for fixing problems from the CEO and the leadership team to the employees in a form that we had not envisioned with the original idea. Simply by allowing questions to be asked, we had improved the likelihood that answers would emerge—from someone, somewhere. By being open and acknowledging the imperfections that existed in the company, we had shifted the conversation away from what was wrong to what could be done about it. Although the list of issues to be fixed never gets shorter, the problems we face today are not the ones we faced five years ago. The U&I portal continues to attract significant traffic every week, and has become a great source of information that helps me to understand where we are and what issues we need to address next.

There were other experiments in increasing transparency. Some went horribly wrong; some went surprisingly right. We never, however, fell in love with any of these ideas in and of themselves. We just focused on the results, which seemed to show that the sun was shining bright and strong and we were now ready for real change. Or so I thought at that time.

Explaining to Customers Why
They Come Second

As we were working on building trust internally, we continued to focus on developing new business, new strategies, and new solutions for our customers. Part of our eventual success with our customers can be traced to a meeting we held in February 2006 with three hundred customer representatives, most of them chief information officers (CIOs). They journeyed to Delhi from around the world.

The idea for the meeting came from my conversations with customers. I wanted to know whether they were really getting value from our EFCS approach. I wanted to better understand their relationships with other vendors. Did our customers trust their vendors? Did the vendors provide enough transparency for them? And I wanted our customers to know that although we said we put them second, they were, of course, central to our business, and that EFCS was meant to create tremendous value for them, as well as for us.

In this meeting, I wanted to expand the idea of transparency. So we did a Mirror Mirror session with the customers and shared with them what we thought we needed to change at HCLT. We explained the challenges that lay ahead and the path we wished to follow to address these issues and to create higher value for them.

We also saw the meeting as an opportunity to continue increasing transparency with our employees. Why not broadcast the event so that our employees could listen to the conversation and see just how serious we were about EFCS? And that's exactly what we did. While three hundred HCLT customers gathered in a conference room, thousands of HCLT employees gathered in front of their computers to watch and listen. It was a level of transparency that HCLT employees had never seen before. On that day, many fence sitters became transformers.

During the two-day meeting, we introduced a number of speakers—including analysts, customer experts, and HCLT leaders. We covered a wide variety of topics, such as the changing needs of customers, the changing aspirations of our people, and increasing demands on CIOs. We talked about new technology trends, privacy issues, the world economy, the emergence of India and China as big consumer markets, and changes in consumer behavior that were causing the emergence of new business-to-business and business-to-consumer models. We argued that these issues would require more than just a few innovative ideas; they would need a fundamental change in the models of partnership.

And then I presented to the customer audience our Employees First, Customers Second philosophy. I talked at length about the concept and how it was already benefiting our customers and leading to better, stronger relationships.

I closed the meeting by assuring the audience that EFCS did not mean we considered customers second-class citizens. "You face extraordinary business challenges that will drive new IT challenges in the years ahead," I said. "You need integrated solutions for complex processes. You need transparency and flexibility. You need to increase your agility. In order for you to accomplish these things, you need to enter into value-based relationships with IT suppliers who understand your business goals and can align their technology solutions with them."

I continued: "To be that kind of supplier, we at HCLT believe that we must create a whole new business model. We must change the way we build and sustain value in our partnerships with you, our customers. These partnerships will require us all to think far beyond the technology solutions themselves. Success lies in how the solutions are implemented and the sustained business benefit you derive. We believe that by putting our employees first—doing everything we can to enable those people who bring real value to you—we will serve you far better than ever before. Our new approach does not mean we will take our customers for granted. Never. What we want to do is unleash the power of our bright minds. We want them to align themselves with your challenges and become your enablers and facilitators. We intend to develop partnerships that are transparent and trusted and will create tremendous value for you and, as a result, for us. That is why Employees First is such an important part of our strategy. To realize its incredible potential, we need not only your understanding and approval, but also your active involvement."

How did our customers respond? Two "yes, but . . ." customers were not convinced about HCLT's new approach, seeing it as too little too late, and canceled their contracts with us. A few fence sitters said, "Sounds interesting. Let's see how it goes." Some, the transformers, loved it and asked, "What do you want us to do to help you?"

On balance, our customers were more understanding than I had expected. With just one meeting, we had engaged several large customers as active participants in this change, and our employees, watching at their desks, realized that the new approach was the right one. Customers began to see that by putting employees first, our goal was to create more value for them, the customers, not less—that in our reversing of the standard equation, they would, in fact, come out ahead.

Our customers began to breathe more easily. They smiled. Sometimes even at me.

Winning Big Ones Against the Big Boys

As we continued to improve our transparency, we made progress on building trust throughout the organization. I reviewed our progress on Maister's four elements of trust.

Reliability: We were doing better. The online tools helped us improve on that score.

Intimacy: Doing better here also. The endless conversations contributed to that.

Self-orientation: This too was better. Managers were much more visible and engaged than ever before. They had become more skilled at listening.

Credibility: Not so good.

What help were transparency and a culture of trust if we couldn't make good on our new business strategy— our goal of becoming a global IT services provider and winning business against the big boys?

In the fall of that year, however, the tide started to turn. We started winning against the global players. The first win was a deal that we closed with Autodesk in November 2005. It was much larger than our previous largest contract and was headed in the right direction in terms of partnership.

Then came the big breakthrough.

In late spring of 2005, we had set our sights on one very large potential deal with a company called DSG International. The company is a conglomerate of retailers of electrical and electronic goods—TVs, laptops, washers, GPS units, iPods, and more—perhaps best known for the Dixons chain based in the United Kingdom. We refer to the conglomerate simply as Dixons.

In Dixons, we thought we saw a perfect opportunity for HCLT. Our new organizational structure enabled us to offer the complete range of services Dixons was looking for, in an integrated and very efficient way. All through the summer and fall, our people worked incredibly hard. They created new tools and templates and processes. They developed wonderful things out of nothing. They put together a brilliant solution that no global player could match.

In mid-January 2006, DSG International announced its choice. Here's how it was reported in the *ZDNet Asia,* a major source of global tech business news: "Kevin O'Byrne, group finance director of DSG international, said, 'This co-sourcing partnership will enhance our capabilities, drive innovation and improve our agility as we build our position as Europe's leading electrical retailer.' "[1]

Partnership. Co-sourcing. Beautiful words. No mention of the words *supplier* or *vendor* or *outsourcer.* Not only was it by far the largest deal that HCLT had made in its history, but it was also the largest IT services outsourcing deal *ever* for *any* Indian company.

Another article, in *EFY Times,* quoted me: "It is because of our people and people practices that we get opportunities like these to demonstrate the true value which HCLT-ites deliver to our customers."[2]

Put employees first, and customers will follow.

And indeed they did. Just six months after the Dixons win, we entered into a five-year, multimillion-dollar, multiservice outsourcing deal with Teradyne, a leading supplier of automatic test equipment in the United States, beating the global giants that were with us in the race. Chuck Ciali, CIO of Teradyne, underlined our partnership model as a key differentiator. "We selected HCLT on the basis of its breadth of experience with global customers in the hi-tech manufacturing industry, its partnership approach and the transparency in its engagement models."[3]

But it was an industry analyst, Eamonn Kennedy, research director at Ovum, who really articulated the success of our new strategy for all the world to hear: "To all the remaining doubters out there: HCLT has just whipped away your comfort blanket. This engagement is proof that Indian-based outsourcers have what it takes to beat the established players."[4]

In the twelve months after the Blueprint meeting, we won five large outsourcing deals, worth a total of $700 million, all of them in competition with the Big Four global IT providers. The industry took notice. The buzz about HCLT had begun. "HCL Technologies is disruptive and bears watching," read the headline of an IDC report. "HCL may very well be one of the contenders to lead the IT services world of the very near future."[5] And this from *The Economist*: "IBM and the other multinationals are becoming increasingly nervous about the fifth-biggest Indian outsourcer, HCL Technologies."[6]

The Power of Catalysts to Create a Culture of Change

Now, before going on to the next chapter, keep in mind that we did *not* have all this activity planned out carefully in advance. Yes, I had the big strategy sketched out in my mind, but things were even more fluid and improvisational than I have described them here.

In hindsight, I see that within a broad plan, we were trying a variety of things, and that these ideas and initiatives (the ones that worked, anyway) brought about a specific positive change. More important, they served as catalysts for further change, beyond the original intent. One small change in the chemistry of the organization could provoke a very powerful, and often an unexpected, escalation and acceleration of even greater change.

This was true of sharing the financial information and for U&I, as well as other activities we pursued. In retrospect, I believe that I was driven by three very strong convictions:

- That Mirror Mirror, which had started as an exercise, could and should become a sustained approach and an institutionalized way of thinking

- That trust was essential for us to execute on our strategy and that it could only be created by going far beyond conventional notions of transparency

- That just a few catalyst ideas, like the idea of the Amsterdam window, can ignite a lot of change

Catalysts are simple actions, rather than elaborate programs of organizational transformation change that plod on for years and years, and they can help transform a locked-up culture into one that is constantly changing. I do not suggest that the catalysts we employed at HCLT are those that others should employ. I only urge you to find your own catalysts, push them hard, and then find new ones and push them even harder still.

CHAPTER THREE

Inverting the Organizational Pyramid

Building a Structure for Change

Suddenly, it seemed, we had finished all our tasks!

We had looked into the mirror and confronted reality. We had dramatically increased our transparency and addressed the issue of trust. We had won a few big decisive deals and were winning new ones with encouraging regularity. There was rejoicing throughout the land of HCLT. Any day now, it seemed, we could declare victory and rest on our laurels!

That was exactly my fear.

I worried that the gains and changes we had made were not big enough or deep enough—that inch by inch, decision by decision, action by action, we might slowly and inexorably slide back down the mountain we had only just begun to climb.

The more I thought about what we had accomplished, the more it seemed that we had successfully created an environment that was *ready* for change. Such an environment is very different from a company that has actually *made* a change and even farther from a company that has created a long-lasting transformation.

I did not know what our next move should be. So, as I often do, I looked to my past for some guidance. I remembered the geography teacher I'd had in grade school. Our school sat at the edge of the foothills. One clear day, she led us outside and pointed to the Himalayas in the distance.

"What do you see beyond the mountains?" she asked.

We had no idea, so we made up all kinds of answers. She asked the question again and again. Finally, we had to admit that we did not know.

"Good," she said. "That's the right answer. Now let's go inside and see if we can find out."

At HCLT, as we looked toward the end of 2006, I did not know what lay beyond the mountains for us.

I had a pretty good sense of the lay of the land on this side of the mountains, however. Just as we had discussed at the Blueprint meeting, customers were increasingly frustrated with their IT vendors and wanted to get more value for the significant amounts of money they were spending on information technology. Moreover, their frustrations could be turned into a huge opportunity for HCLT. I also saw that we could not yet seize that opportunity, because we were really not much different from the vendors who were causing the frustration. Yes, we had enjoyed a lot of success recently. But winning a few deals would not transform the entire company.

I realized that we had to do much more than fiddle around with our current processes, which made me think back to a summer job I had held during my student days. There, I learned something that I now saw as relevant to our position at HCLT.

A Lesson from the Poultry Farm

During my school years, I took a summer job on a poultry farm near my home. I worked with a number of friends, and our job was to gather eggs from the henhouses, which were on one side of the farm, and carry them to the storage sheds on the other side. The poultry manager gave us detailed instructions about how we were to do the job. Each of us would gather a basket of eggs in one of the henhouses, carry it to one of the storage sheds, then go back for more, crisscrossing the farmyard until all the eggs had been collected and deposited in the storage sheds.

We followed orders for a day or two. Then, being pretty smart young kids, we decided this egg-handling methodology had its limitations. It was slow, boring, and inefficient. We got paid once the job was done, not by the number of hours worked. If we could deliver all the eggs in a shorter time, we could get off work earlier and spend our free time playing soccer or doing whatever else we liked.

We started experimenting. What if we carried more eggs per handful? What if we used one of the henhouses as a central depot, collecting all the eggs there first and then making our trips to the storage sheds? What if we divided the labor—some of the workers collecting while others delivered?

After about two weeks of trying every method we could think of, it became clear that each method had its advantages and disadvantages, but none of them really made much difference. We were still carrying eggs in the same way that people had been carrying eggs for decades, probably centuries, maybe even millennia. We grew tired of experimenting and went back to doing the job as it always had been done. To make the work more tolerable, we joked and talked about what we would do after we got off work. Maybe we'd play a cricket match. Or maybe we'd go home and listen to the Beatles.

On my last day of work that summer, I had a revelation about the job. I realized that tinkering with the process of egg carrying or just trying harder would never change the fundamental nature of the work or the operation of the poultry farm. We were stuck in an archaic structure, and until that changed, nothing else would or could change.

The same was true of our experiments at HCLT, including U&I and the sharing of financial information. We had tinkered with the process and put ourselves in the mood for change, but we were still carrying our eggs in pretty much the same way we always had.

It seemed to me that we now had to look more deeply at how our farm was structured. We had to find ways to build our EFCS approach into our organizational structure in a way that was fundamental and not easily reversed.

The Old Pyramid in a New Landscape

As I've said, the organization at HCLT, like that at so many other companies, was a traditional pyramid structure. There were the senior people on top; a thick layer of middle managers and enabling functions such as finance, human resources, training and development, quality, and administration in the middle; and the frontline workers, who had the least power and influence, on the bottom.

The command-and-control approach has characterized large organizations for centuries. Monarchies, armies, and religious institutions have grown, expanded, and dominated their competitors by creating rigid hierarchies that serve a supreme leader. The structure worked equally well in the industrial economy when it first emerged.

The value zone of industrial companies is deep inside the organization, in the R&D centers and the manufacturing plants. Everything else could be seen as important but not essential to competitive differentiation and market success.

For many years, IT had essentially been a manufacturing industry. The value zone lay—just as it had in automobiles, appliances, and aerospace—in hardware design and manufacture. Every company was trying to create the faster chip, the better user interface, the smarter feature, and offer it all at the lowest possible price.

The rise of the knowledge economy, however, has changed all that. As I had realized from my very first days as CEO at HCLT (particularly from some of those conversations with customers), the value zone no longer lay in the technology itself and certainly not in any particular hardware or software technology. Customers could choose among many options, all of which would likely enable them to achieve their goals if implemented well.

Something had to be different, then, about the way the technologies were brought together and implemented for each customer. Something more had to be changed about how we delivered our services.

Four Trends in Information Technology

In order to change the *how*, we had to think carefully about the changes in the global IT landscape and develop a strategy that made sense for what was happening around us.

For HCLT in 2005, the IT world was characterized by four major trends.

First, as we had realized in our assessment of our point A during the Mirror Mirror exercise, business was growing more complex and IT was becoming more central to business strategy. Consequently, the position of chief information officer (CIO) had much more power and prominence than in the past.

Second, the IT industry was valued the most when it developed innovative technologies that could help make business processes faster, cheaper, and more available and that offered the analytics that CIOs and other company leaders needed to drive better decisions. But adopting such technologies also increased the implementation complexity of the hardware and application solutions involved.

Third, the increased complexity of the customer's business, combined with the increasing complexity of solutions (usually sourced from multiple vendors), made it necessary for customers to focus on execution and implementation. They needed to avoid being overly seduced by the hype around the latest innovation. The implication was that customers would increasingly be looking for solutions that were customized to their specific needs but that could be built, as much as possible, on standard technologies. In other words, this value zone would become more critical in the future, because that's where the customization and implementation got done.

Finally, system integrators—companies that gather technologies and solutions from a variety of vendors and, theoretically, make them all work seamlessly together—were coming under increasing pressure from their customers to work to a much higher standard of performance than ever before and to show more success in creating unique solutions. But because the different teams involved usually belonged to different hierarchies, those of the system integrator's company and of the customer's company, the organizational hierarchies often got in their way. As a result, greenfield projects often ran into difficulty, took longer than planned, or could not ultimately deliver the hoped-for business benefits.

The Opportunity and a Strategy to Seize It

We knew that in those trends lay our opportunity: to define HCLT as an IT provider focused on aligning solutions with business strategy, a company that, through the use of innovative tools and technologies (but no more innovative than necessary), enabled customers to cut down the cycle times in their most critical business processes, including these:

Order to cash: from the moment of accepting a customer order to the receipt of payment for delivery of the order

Desire to hire: from the definition of an open job position to filling it

Concept to manufacture: from new-product prototype to finished production unit

In other words, we would shift our focus from the stuff we were selling to the results we could help our customers achieve.

Getting multiple teams to work closely together on a complex business problem is easier said than done, of course. However, it is not really a problem of teamwork. In my experience, when teams focus on an objective, they eventually find ways to collaborate. The problem was much more a matter of what we at HCLT call the "Hand of God."

That is to say, the bosses get in the way.

The senior managers, sitting at their lofty remove from the real action, are the ones who can exercise the Hand of God decision that often puts at risk everything that is happening in the value zone. Why? Because bosses genuinely believe that by virtue of their position at the top of the pyramid, they have a better view of the landscape and are the best situated to make decisions that will benefit the entire organization.

This logic is hard to dispute. We do need to consider the forty-thousand-foot view, after all. We need to try to see what lies beyond the mountains. But, I thought, this is the conventional wisdom. This is how our competitors think. It is how our customers expect us all to think. This rationale will not lead us to a new strategy or provoke fundamental change. It will only keep us toting the eggs in the same old baskets.

So, we began to think about some of the questions that were coming through U&I and that were being asked in our town hall meetings—questions like these:

- "I don't understand why I report to this particular manager. He does not really understand my job. What value can he add to what I do?" This interesting question made me think about the link between reporting structure and the creation of value.

- "Why must we spend so much time doing tasks required by the enabling functions? Shouldn't human resources be supporting me, so I can support customers better? They seem to have an inordinate amount of power, considering the value they add to the customer." This question suggested that organizational power should be proportionate to one's ability to add value, rather than by one's position on the pyramid.

- "Many managers have far more influence on how much value I can deliver than the ones I actually report to. But we have no formal connection, no way to evaluate each other. Does that make sense?" No, it did not make sense that a manager's span of hierarchical control should limit his or her influence on those beyond that span.

Nor did it make sense that employees reported to a manager who could not add value to their job or that people who created little value could wield a lot of power.

The more we thought about it, the more we realized that very little about the archaic pyramid made much sense anymore, given the trends we had identified and the aspirations we had defined for ourselves in the IT landscape.

That's when the radical idea of the inverted pyramid came back to my mind. What if we made the boss as accountable to the value zone as the value zone was accountable to the boss? What if we made the boss accountable not just to his or her own team but to all the other team members in that value zone whom the boss may be positively or negatively influencing?

If we could do those things, would they create the kind of fundamental change we were looking for? Would the change ignite the passion of our employees in that value zone? Would they then be driven to deliver far greater value than our competitors could? Would our customers see that was happening, understand it, and value it, too?

Was I dreaming? Possibly. But if so, I was hardly the first person to have followed this train of thought.

C. K. Prahalad, the well-known author and management guru, wrote a book titled *Fortune at the Bottom of the Pyramid*, in which he predicts that "the bottom of the pyramid is going to become the biggest opportunity for innovation in business models."[1] Prahalad is thinking mostly about the commercial opportunities of serving emerging economies with large populations rather than opportunities of corporate structure. Still, the concept has relevance for the way companies organize themselves. The "bottom" represents a huge untapped opportunity for driving customer-focused innovation.

Research by Gallup supports this idea. According to the findings of polls Gallup has conducted over many decades, customers switch from one supplier to another because they are attracted by one of the "four Ps" of marketing—a better *product,* a lower *price*, an attractive *promotion*, or better *placement* (a.k.a. location).

However, the four Ps—as attractive as they may be—will not create a strong and lasting relationship between customer and partner without the fifth P, which stands, of course, for people. Placement, promotion, price—and even product—cannot make up for a lack of engagement, execution, commitment, and close relationships between the people in a customer organization and those in the partner or supplier organization.

So if all this were true, as I believed it was, what implications would it have for the pyramid we called HCLT?

How could we build collaboration into the organizational structure?

Another Lesson from the Family Model

As I have discussed, I believe that the institution of the family has gradually made a transition from a command-and-control hierarchy to a more collaborative enterprise and so can serve as a good model for us to follow. But how has it done so? And what are the main characteristics of this new family unit?

In addition to trust, I realized, one of the most important changes had to do with an issue we were now considering at HCLT: *accountability.* In the traditional family, children were completely accountable to the parents. They were accountable in minor things, such as doing their chores and getting good grades and being polite, and accountable in major things, as well—their educational path, the careers they followed, and who they married.

Now I saw that the accountability had been reversed. Many parents felt accountable to their children. Yes, adults still shouldered the traditional responsibilities of feeding, clothing, and providing shelter for their kids. But they also began to see that their own actions or inactions, behaviors and habits, beliefs and prejudices, had a tremendous potential for influencing their children—in how they did in school and socially; in their mental, physical, and emotional health; and in how they looked at the world. Parents had also begun to make a direct connection between what they themselves did and how their sons and daughters might turn out in the future. Would their children succeed and be happy?

So there was a different kind of accountability going on in the new family.

Obviously, a business organization is different from a family. But it was important to ask why the corporate organization seemed so much more outdated than other structures in our society. Why do so many people disdain corporate structure, in general, and dislike the companies where they work in particular? Conversely, why do they so revere the family unit, even if theirs is dysfunctional? What makes people believe in democracy, even if they're disappointed with the leaders currently in power?

We began to think that we needed to make HCLT more like the modern family. But we did not want to make a sudden and all-encompassing change, because that would destabilize the company and cause too much disruption. Nor did we want to abandon all hierarchy, because formal structure provides the discipline and accountability that organizations need in order to function efficiently.

We just wanted to make a small change in how things worked and to do so in a way that might have great and long-lasting impact.

Reverse Accountability

We knew that we had to define the term *reverse accountability* very carefully.

We did not want to turn this into a discussion of individuals or specific positions. We were not talking about making executives accountable to frontline workers. We did not expect that our senior vice president of engineering would have to get his time sheet signed by the cafeteria worker.

Reverse accountability simply meant that we wanted to get certain elements of the hierarchy to be more accountable to the value zone. In particular, we looked at three categories of positions: the enabling functions; the managerial chain of command all the way to the CEO; and the influencers who are not part of the hierarchy but are critical to achieving the desired wow in the value zone.

The Power of the Enabling Functions

We started by looking at the enabling functions. We found that the employees in the value zone were as accountable to finance, human resources, training and development, quality, administration, and other enabling functions as they were to their immediate managers.

Although these functions were supposed to be supporting the employees in the value zone, the reality was sometimes different. Policies, which were supposed to be transparent and consistent across the organization, were often interpreted differently by different managers in different parts of the company, and the reasons for the deviations were not always clear to the employees. This made life especially difficult for new employees who were not well-connected in the organization; when they had a request or question, they could not be sure who to approach or how long an issue might take to resolve. As a result, many employees found that the best approach was to put on their best smiles, say "Please," and start praying.

The employees had virtually no influence over the enabling functions. So, if there was a problem, the people generally had to look upward in the pyramid—to their manager or their manager's manager—for help, for that Hand of God decision.

As a result, the managers became go-betweens and arbitrators and, from those roles, derived power. The manager was the one to whom the employee had to make supplication. The manager picked up the phone to make the all-important call to the enabler or someone even higher up. The manager negotiated. And the manager delivered the final answer, satisfactory or not.

Therein lay power, not value; bottlenecks, not facilitation.

"What have the enabling functions done to help you create more value in the value zone?" When I asked that question, I usually got silence from the employees. Was the picture really as bad as employees painted it? Perhaps not. But the employees' perception of the enabling functions was negative, and we found this to be the case in many other organizations.

So was there a way to reverse the accountability between the enabling functions and the employees in the value zone? We kicked the idea around at length. At last, a team of our bright sparks came up with an inspired idea: the *Smart Service Desk*.

The Smart Service Desk Concept

The Smart Service Desk (SSD) was based on a problem management system we already had in place for our customers.

That system had been effective and worked simply. Whenever a customer issue arose, we would create an electronic ticket that detailed the problem and tracked its progress as it worked its way toward a solution. When the issue was resolved, the appropriate manager in the responsible department closed the ticket. This is a fairly standard procedure, one used by companies in many industries that have lots of customer contact, such as airlines, hotels, and car rental companies.

The idea was to create a similar system to resolve internal issues between the enabling functions and employees. Whenever an employee had a problem or needed information, he or she could open a ticket that would be directed to the appropriate department for handling. Each ticket would have a deadline for resolution. The system would be transparent so that all could see the contents of the tickets and where they were in the process. And the employee who had opened the ticket would be the one to determine whether the resolution had been satisfactory, or if the issue had been resolved at all.

I floated the idea with members of the enabling function leadership teams. Some took to the idea right away. Many, however, voiced their vehement "yes, buts."

"We're not merely power brokers and go-betweens," they said. "That characterization is unfair. We work the hardest of anyone. And we are the least appreciated. This system will send a signal to the whole company that we are the ones who need to be monitored. That our work is unnecessary. That we are not good enough."

I listened to these views and then asked the leaders to discuss the idea with their teams.

A few days later, the managers started reporting back to me. They had interesting expressions on their faces when they said, with some resignation, "OK. We've changed our minds. Let's go for it."

"What changed your minds?" I asked.

They started by saying rather predictable things about putting employees first and increasing trust and pushing for greater transparency. But as I probed deeper, a more important reason came out.

"Well, with the ticket system, we will be able to measure *our* performance, share it with people, and change their perception about us," one of the managers finally explained. "That way, we can finally prove what we have been saying all along: that we are the ones who work the hardest and that the problem usually lies with the employee, not the other way around!"

I had not thought of it that way. I began to suspect that this small catalyst might have the larger effect that we were hoping for.

How the Ticket Works

The internal SSD approach works much the same way that a customer service desk works. An employee can open a ticket for one of three categories of issues—a problem, a query, or a work request—and the ticket can be directed to any one of the enabling functions, including HR, finance, administration, training and development, IT/IS teams, transport, and others. Employees can also open a ticket on most members of senior management, including me.

Once the employee has filled out the ticket, the system automatically assigns it to a support executive in the appropriate department. He or she will investigate the issue and take any action necessary to resolve it. The support executive commits to a set of accountability metrics for each ticket, including how long it should take to complete. The metrics are based on a number of factors, including the complexity and urgency of the request.

If the support executive does not resolve the issue within the specified time, the ticket is automatically sent to the executive's manager, and so on up the line.

The entire SSD process is transparent so that an employee can check the status of his or her ticket at any time. Once the issue is resolved, the support executive closes the ticket. If, however, the employee who raised it is not satisfied with the resolution, he or she can refuse the closed status of the ticket. It will remain open and the clock will keep ticking. The employee can also rate the quality of service provided by the support executive.

One other interesting aspect of the SSD is that the employee's manager is always in the know about the status of the ticket (except those that concern an issue related to the relationship between the employee and manager). Consequently, the manager can't claim, "I had no idea this was a problem!" The moment a ticket is opened, the manager gets an e-mail explaining what's going on.

This has a very interesting secondary effect. I have seen managers reach out to the employee who has opened a ticket to ask whether there are other concerns beyond those expressed in the ticket. This can begin a deeper conversation about problems, challenges, frustrations, and possible solutions. Smart managers realize that the SSD ticket, like so many of the EFCS initiatives, is a catalyst— a way to bring about change beyond the original, intended purpose.

The Reaction

News of SSD had the desired effect. It sent a fresh, cool breeze through the pyramid of HCLT. People had a variety of reactions and queries:

- Can employees open tickets on the enabling functions? On managers?

- Will managers be evaluated on their handling of these tickets?

- Will employees have the power to reopen a ticket if they are not satisfied?

- Can employees open a ticket on the CEO?

To help introduce the system, we ran an internal communications campaign that outlined the benefits of this new way of doing things. We also ensured that the company leaders showed their support for the project. I personally sent hundreds of e-mails to people throughout the organization testifying to the benefits of SSD and linking it to our company's larger objectives and vision.

We encouraged everybody in the enabling functions to politely refuse any requests for problem resolution that did *not* come through the SSD system.

At first, people continued to walk along in the old ways. When they had a problem, they picked up the phone or went to the office of a manager to have a conversation.

But, within a few weeks, as the system gained acceptability and people saw that it worked, the number of tickets shot up.

Soon, people were opening tickets at an average of thirty thousand per month (at a time when there was a total of about thirty thousand employees in the company). This seemed like a huge success. We were resolving thousands of transactions each month, at an amazing rate, the majority of which would previously not have been resolved at all or even brought to anyone's attention. Think of all the issues that had previously gone unaddressed and now were being attended to. People were embracing the system. It was a victory for honesty, transparency, and openness!

But wait a minute. We thought more carefully about the numbers. If we had an average of more than thirty thousand tickets a month, many of which concerned problems we had been unaware of, didn't that suggest that we had a *lot* of problems at HCLT? Should we be celebrating the fact that so much was in such disarray?

I wondered if perhaps we were fighting the battle in the wrong way.

Going for Zero Tickets

After the SSD had been in place for a few months, I attended an open house with about a hundred HCLT employees who were working on a customer project in the United Kingdom.

I made a few informal comments about the ticket system and how I thought it was contributing to the reversal of accountability and then asked for questions and comments.

A young woman, whom I'll call Irene, spoke up. "Vineet, I have a question," she said. "When something goes wrong at a customer site, what does the customer want to know about the problem?"

Well, I thought I knew the answer she was looking for, but I decided to have her tell me and the rest of the people in the audience.

"Please explain, Irene," I said. "What does the customer want to know?"

"Two things," she said. "First, they want to know how fast we responded to the problem. The second thing they want to know is what caused the problem in the first place. Why did it happen?"

"Yes. Responding fast is good, but . . ."

"But not having it happen again is even better," Irene said, cutting me off. "The same is true with our internal system. Think about it. Every time an employee opens a trouble ticket, it implies that he or she is not happy, that there is an issue. The question is, why does the employee have an issue at all? Why can't we have a company with *no* issues?"

This comment struck me as incredibly important.

"Wow," I said to Irene. "So what you are saying is that the enabling functions should be in the business of *zero* tickets?"

"Yes, of course, that is what I am saying," she said, sounding a bit exasperated. "The way it works now, the enabling functions are evaluated on how quickly they respond to a trouble ticket and how well it is resolved. But they are not evaluated on whether they have fixed the problem for good. The system does not encourage them to be proactive. Just reactive."

I was silent for a moment. We had developed the SSD system for a good reason: to change the accountabilities in our hierarchy and to begin to turn the pyramid upside down. Now the system seemed to offer us an even greater benefit: a way to identify long-standing issues so we could fix them for good. That would really take reverse accountability up a notch.

After that meeting, we started looking at proactivity in the enabling functions. In addition to quick resolution of tickets, could we have a goal of zero ticket days and zero ticket issues?

In the weeks since we had established the SSD, we had already gathered a lot of data. Now, by analyzing it carefully, we began to see patterns. We could see which issues were the most common, which employee zones produced which types of tickets the most frequently, and which enabling functions had chronic problems and pain points.

Then we looked at how these issues could be addressed. We found three root causes of most problems: an unsatisfactory policy, inadequate or unclear communication, and poor execution or implementation of a satisfactory policy or process.

We asked the enabling functions to start looking at the most frequent problems, determine their root causes, and find a way to fix them. Rewrite the policy. Improve communications. Or change a process to improve implementation.

The goal for each function was to reach a zero-ticket week.

In moving toward that goal, employees began to see that problems they had struggled with for years and that had taken up too much time and energy were disappearing. After a short time, we started tracking the leading indicators that caused the number of these tickets to rise. Over the years, the process and the system have become very effective and sophisticated.

SSD also had an impact on employees' attitudes toward the company more generally. A few years after we initiated SSD, we were ranked number one in an employee satisfaction survey, and I came across an interesting analysis of how SSD had helped us score so well. In HCLT, as in most business organizations, the response from the enabling function to an employee's request had varied, depending on who the employee was and how much power he or she wielded. This variance frustrated frontline employees, who believed they worked just as hard as people who were senior to them in the organization, but who did not necessarily get the same respect as the higher-ups and who may also have received different, and less helpful, responses from people in the enabling functions. The SSD initiative essentially leveled the playing field. It didn't matter where the employee was in the hierarchy, his or her issue would be heard. This reduced the frustration and fundamentally changed the employees' perception of the company, which significantly increased their satisfaction at work— one probable reason we received the number one ranking in the survey.

Disrupting the Zone of Control: The 360-Degree Survey

SSD sent a pleasant ripple of change running through the pyramid, but did not come close to toppling it. That was fine. As I said, we did not wish to cause complete and immediate disruption. But it was clear that the pyramid needed to be rocked a bit more vigorously.

To further our efforts in reversing the accountability, we would have to cast our net wider, to include the managers of the enabling functions as well as executives up the hierarchy in the line functions, in fact, all the way up to the office of the CEO, including me. To do so, we had to deal with the issue of *control*.

What is the source of the manager's control? It does not come simply from a position in the hierarchy, a title, or a job description. Some senior managers gain control through fear rather than through respect. They ultimately have the power to say, "This employee is good, this one is bad. This one gets promoted, this one does not. This one gets resources, this one gets none. This employee stays, this one goes."

How could we change this reliance on control? What we needed was another catalyst—the blue ocean droplet—to create a new mindset.

We found it in our performance review process. At the time, our standard process was as traditional as our pyramidal structure. Although we used a 360-degree survey, each manager was reviewed by a relatively small number of people—those who inhabited the manager's zone of control, including his or her superior and immediate colleagues and those who reported directly to the manager.

In other words, the review was conducted by members of a kind of good old boys' club. Because they all had to review each other, they would scratch each other's back, give each other high marks, say only nice things, and ignore problems, and everything would continue as it had for years. Most fooled themselves into believing that they, and all their colleagues, were doing a jolly good job. Even if they did get some developmental feedback, it was more likely to be ignored than acted upon.

Moreover, the performance metrics were all about activities within the manager's immediate span of control. There was nothing in the 360-degree review about contributing to the value zone. So, if asked about value, a manager could easily say, "Oh, well, I am way up here in the chain of command, and the value zone is way over there. I can have no effect on that. There is nothing I can do."

Perhaps a change in the way we did the 360-degree review could bring about the desired results. We set some of our bright sparks to thinking about it. Within a few days, they came up with three important modifications to the process: openness, expansion to a broader group and to people beyond the evaluee's span of control, and its use as a developmental rather than an evaluative tool. Would it make a difference?

Opening Up the 360

Let's start with the problems associated with the traditional 360-degree review as it is practiced in many business organizations. In most companies, the manager to be evaluated chooses the respondents, which means that the manager tends to select people who will be biased in favor of his or her performance. Even so, participation in 360-degree surveys is generally low, because subordinates see no win for them in evaluating their bosses. And as the results of most surveys are kept confidential, the participants don't know if their feedback was similar to that of others or if their suggestions have been acted upon. And finally, the manager's superior often disregards the 360 altogether, because of his or her own concerns and perceptions.

Why not open it up? We decided to allow *anyone* who had given feedback to a manager to see the results of that manager's 360. This had not been the case before. The rationale was that by giving authorization to all the participants to view the manager's report, they would feel empowered and would be more likely to participate. In order to ensure the confidentiality, anonymity, and accurate data encryption of the process, we decided to bring in a third party to audit and certify the survey. Only with an outside party keeping an eye on the process would people feel comfortable enough to give honest and candid feedback. We believed that as a result, managers would celebrate positive results with their teams, which would facilitate learning and development. Finally, the manager's boss would become far less powerful in the process, as this person would be just one voice among many. The team in the value zone would be determining the results of the survey, which would be one more step toward inverting the pyramid.

I knew this was an extremely delicate issue and began asking for feedback from my leadership team. They were quick to see where this might be heading and the benefits we could achieve. We did have a few "yes, buts" that helped us think it through and understand all that could go wrong. The concerns included these:

- Is it about popularity?

- Can I work with the team if I get a low score?

- How will I exercise control on my team after this?

- What if my rating is low because I make tough decisions?

- What if I do not want to share my results?

- Will this influence my appraisal and bonus?

These were all valid questions we would have to grapple with. I knew that it would be impossible to force managers to make their reviews public. That would be pushing the envelope too far. I could only encourage them to do so. The best way to do that was for me to lead the way. So I posted my 360-degree survey result for all the company to see. Once I did this, other senior managers followed suit.

When you think about it, how could they not? If the feedback was positive, all would be well. They would feel good. They would be motivated. They would strive for even better scores next time. What's more, they would be able to see the results of their colleagues and superiors. They would become competitive with one another, which would lead to still further improvement.

If the feedback was negative, however, the manager would at last be forced to face the reality of unsatisfactory performance and how he or she was viewed by others. It would be a kind of personal Mirror Mirror exercise, and they had all seen how powerful and useful that could be. What's more, the managers knew that in a culture of trust and of acceptance of change, a negative review would be seen differently than it might have been a year earlier—as an opportunity for improvement rather than as a mark of failure.

Besides, if a manager chose *not* to share the performance review, people would notice and would automatically assume the person had something to hide. And, given people's tendency to assume that the bad is far worse than it usually is, hiding the result—even if it was good—would be much worse for the manager than revealing a negative one.

Gradually, the "yes, buts" fell away and people increasingly participated in the open 360-degree. If we had not engaged the leadership team in discussion about the process beforehand, there would have been a high probability of failure. The key to the success of the open 360-degree has been the willingness of managers to use the feedback to bring about a change in their management style.

Happy Feet: Expansion to a Broader Group

As the open 360-degree caught on, however, we began to see that the process was not as open as it seemed, or as it could be. We were still essentially following the traditional practice by restricting and defining who was eligible to give feedback to whom. That meant that most of the respondents operated within the same area as the person they were evaluating. This reinforced the boundaries between the parts of the pyramid. But we were trying to change all that. We wanted to encourage people who operated across these boundaries. How could we recognize and encourage their behavior?

We decided to add a new feature to the open 360-degree instrument; we called it *Happy Feet.*

We opened the performance review process to all our employees whom a manager might affect or influence. (This meant about 1,500 people in 2005, and 3,500 in 2009.) Any employee could choose to do a 360-degree evaluation of any of the managers they believed had an influence—positive or negative—on their ability to do their job. It didn't matter how long the employee had been with HCLT—a month or a decade—or what their reporting relationship was with the manager.

As you might imagine, the idea of a much-broadened 360-degree performance review raised a lot of "yes, buts" from the managers. And again, the objections were valid and useful ones.

"I don't think this kind of 360-degree survey will produce reliable results," one manager said to me. "You are asking people who I don't know and who have never met me to evaluate my performance. How is this possible? How does it make any sense?"

"Have you read a book called *The Wisdom of Crowds*?" I asked.

When he replied no, I told him about the book. In it, author James Surowiecki of *The New Yorker* talks about how wisdom resides in groups of people, the crowd, far more than in any one individual. The many know more than the few. Collective wisdom outshines individual judgment.

"Maybe," the manager replied. "But won't outliers skew the results? What if one reviewer gives exceptionally harsh marks? Or what if a group of employees bands together and deliberately tries to influence the review? What if employees randomly decide to make comments on managers they have nothing to do with? I can see all kinds of ways to game this system."

"All of those things are possible," I said. "It is a question of trust. Over the past few months, we have all worked very hard to create a culture of trust here at HCLT. This is another way to show that we trust each other. I believe that most employees will play this fairly. Remember, they are also reviewed annually by their managers and they, too, want to trust that their manager will review them fairly. So if they can trust us, can't we trust them? Yes, I am sure there will be a few employees who will rate some managers in the extreme—rating them far worse or better than they actually are—but there will be few such employees. And that is the beauty of the crowd. Because so many people will be participating, the scores given by the outliers will not significantly skew the evaluation of the larger group."

I heard another objection to the extended 360-degree survey from many managers.

"Don't you see that the popular managers will get the highest ratings?" one manager asked. "The managers who are more disciplined, or less outgoing, or more private—even if they are more effective—will get lower marks. That would not be fair."

"Unlikely," I said. "The survey questions will not be about which manager you like the most or which one you would like to work with. You are not taking the manager home to marry, after all. The answer to the problem you raise lies in getting the questions right. If we are trying to maximize the value zone, then the questions have to relate to that effort."

And so we designed a survey that asked questions like these:

- Does this manager help you enhance the value you are delivering to the customer?

- After discovering that you have a problem, does this manager help you define the problem and help you identify its solution?

- When you approach the manager with a problem, does he or she respond by offering solutions or resolving the issues involved?

- If you can't reach the solutions on your own, does the manager enable you to reach out to other people in the organization who help you achieve the solutions?

Again, the actual practice put most of the objections to rest. As there was no restriction on who could give feedback to any manager, the traditional hierarchy was weakened. People who worked outside the boundaries of the pyramid were recognized, encouraged, and rewarded. The public acknowledgement of the value contributed by these people set an example for the rest of the organization and served as a pat on the back for them.

Replacing Zones of Control with Spans of Influence

The open 360-degree survey with Happy Feet had other remarkable effects on the organization. It started to significantly redefine the important zones within our company—emphasizing spans of results-based influence rather than traditional structure-based zones of control.

How did this happen? Let's say that your title is vice president of operations and several hundred people report to you, but only a small percentage of them deliver feedback on you. That shows that your span of influence does not match your zone of control.

Why? Is it that the crowd doesn't have any knowledge of you? That they don't know what you stand for? That you're not enabling them in their quest to create value? That they think you're ineffectual? That they just don't care?

Whatever the reason, the low response rate shows that you have a small span of influence in comparison to your zone of control. More than any other aspect of the survey, this finding galvanized the organization. People saw that the zone of control had become largely irrelevant. It is the span of influence that really matters.

This one really shook the foundations of the pyramid. People began to reach out to others who had never been in their good old boys' club before—both inside and outside their traditional zone of control. They wanted to expand their influence, make a positive contribution, and further push change.

Evaluation as a Developmental Tool

The final modification we made to the 360-degree survey was to redefine it as a developmental tool rather than one of evaluation. It would be a way for the manager to gain useful feedback about his or her performance—feedback that we could use to help the person change.

Note that as an organization, we decided to disconnect the 360-degree survey from the human resources department and its activities. Although the HR group continued to conduct performance appraisals and manage compensation for the manager, the results of the 360-degree process were not taken into consideration in those discussions. The process instead was driven by a new entity called the Talent Transformation and Intrapreneurship Development team. The 360 report served as a starting point for a discussion with managers about their own set of professional development goals. The managers did not have to engage in this process; the choice was always left to them.

In 2009, we further refined the developmental aspect of the 360-degree survey and called it Feedforward. The respondent can identify three critical competencies for the person being reviewed, mark each as "strength" or "development area," and suggest some simple, specific steps the person might take to improve. The section is optional, and the results are kept strictly confidential. The manager is the only one who sees a consolidated view of the results; the names of the feedback providers are not revealed.

Thinking of feedback as a method of development rather than one of judgment or evaluation proved critical to our ability to move away from the command-and-control environment toward one of trust, alignment, and a focus on the qualities and actions that could help people in the value zone.

These changes to our 360-degree process convinced many skeptics within the organization about EFCS, and they were beginning to see that we truly believed in it. Employees were happy that their voices were being heard and their feedback was seen as important. The younger managers in particular loved the honest feedback because it helped them improve their performance and develop their skills faster. My senior leadership team saw how much positive energy the revised process released throughout the organization and used it to create more value in the value zone.

Even managers who consistently received poor feedback benefitted from the process. They came to realize that their strengths simply did not lie in management and they would be better off as individual contributors. Managers with consistently good feedback were able to widen their spans of influence well beyond their zones of control because people throughout the organization knew they were held in high regard.

Keep Talking

It is very important to understand that throughout the transformation at HCLT, and especially during the first few years, we communicated constantly, in a variety of formats, to employees throughout the organization. The communication of an initiative was often as important as the initiative itself. My leadership team was very involved in our communications and marketing efforts, and we spent a lot of time talking about how and when to communicate and what the important messages should be.

I remember one discussion about a major presentation we were planning to make to all employees throughout HCLT—not just the managers or the people in the value zone, but everyone—about EFCS. The Employee Communications team, which had many of our bright sparks as members, wanted me to talk to everyone about the EFCS concept, how we were implementing it through activities like U&I and SSD, how we planned to restructure the company to better enable employees, and our five-year transformation plan.

"OK," I said. "But why should we do this? What is in it for the employee?"

The team members gave me some grandiose answers about sharing in the long-range vision of the company. I asked them again. "Yes, but what do the employees want to know from us? What do they really care about?"

They gave more answers about the changing landscape of IT and helping the company transform itself. I asked the same question four or five more times, and at last the team ran out of answers.

"Just keep in mind," I said, "that when we communicate to the general employee population about organizational changes, the messages must be relevant to them, and those messages may be different from the ones that are relevant to managers or to customers. Our employees are not so concerned about the 'whats' of our IT landscape or about corporate transformation and initiatives. They care about how this affects them personally—what it means to them, their careers, and their families. So the emphasis of our communication should be more about what they consider important rather than a forum to market our initiatives."

My colleagues looked at me as if I were throwing cold water on their idea of a big, company-wide meeting, but I wasn't, really.

"Let me tell you a story," I said, "about making assumptions about what people want."

A Story of Making a Wrong Assumption

I told them about my first school, which had been founded by nuns, in my hometown of Pantnagar. The teachers of the school believed strongly in social service. One of our activities was to go door to door and collect old clothes that we would then distribute to people who lived in the slums, which were fairly close to school.

My young colleagues seemed to consider my story a distraction from the discussion at hand, but I kept going.

"When I was about twelve," I said, "I went into the slum with an armful of clothing. There were lots of kids taking what we had to give them, but one boy sat by himself away from the others. He had no interest in the clothes, but kept staring at my schoolbag."

"What did you have in there?" asked Arun, one of my colleagues. (I have changed his name.)

"The boy was pretty shabbily dressed," I said, ignoring Arun's question. "It was cold, so I asked him, 'Do you want a sweater?' 'No,' he said. He kept his eyes fixed on my bag."

"Did he think you had some food in there?" Arun asked.

"No," I said. "At last he asked me, 'What do you have in your bag?' " I opened it up and showed him: books.

'What do you do with them?' the boy asked. 'We read them,' I replied."

"He said, 'Can you please read one to me?'"

The point I was trying to make with the story was that I had made all the wrong assumptions about what the little boy in the slum cared about. I didn't want us to do the same thing with the HCLT employees. I had seen it happen often. We would become so obsessed with what we were giving to our employees, or giving to our customers, that we started believing that that was what the other person truly wanted and needed.

I guess the story made its point. The conversation turned to how we could structure the all-company meeting so that it would focus on what the Employees First strategy and the transformation plan would do for our employees. Would it make them able to work faster? Would they be able to do their jobs better? Would they learn new things? Would their jobs be easier or more enjoyable?

The team soon came up with a name for the meeting—*Directions*—and a format that would involve a series of informal conversations around topics that were the most important in the minds of the employees. We would not be giving our people clothes when they really wanted books.

The Directions Meetings

We held the first of our Directions meetings in late summer of 2006.

We did not want these meetings to feel like the old days of the traditional pyramid, when senior management would appear on stage, make its pronouncements, and leave. I wanted the communications to have a big impact and to make a lasting impression.

So, as I prepared my remarks in advance of the meeting, I remembered a lesson from my MBA days at XLRI—one that also pertained to communication. My very first class was in basic business skills, taught by Father McGrath. He was talking about presentations, and I confess that I was having a hard time paying attention to him. I had just arrived at school after a forty-hour train journey from home. The classroom was very hot. We were on the first floor, and I gazed out the window at the air choked with dust. There were thirty-five or forty of us in the class.

Suddenly, the door burst open with a ferocious bang, and the room filled with shouts. I turned to see ten or fifteen men running and leaping into the classroom, ribbons tied in their hair, faces painted, carrying spears and brandishing knives. I recognized them as Adivasis, tribal people of India. They screamed and dashed around the room, pushing the students, throwing things, and making an uproar. One of them grabbed the student closest to the door, dragged her to the window, and threw her out. Another one rushed to the front of the room, raised his knife, and stabbed Father McGrath. Blood spurted from his stomach as he fell to the floor groaning. We didn't know what to do. And then, after two minutes of mayhem, the Adivasis vanished as quickly as they had appeared.

Everybody in the room looked stunned. Nobody moved. Some of us were still sitting, some standing, and some looked as if they were about to jump out the window. Then Father McGrath stopped groaning, stood up, brushed himself off, and smiled.

"Everyone sit down," he said, calmly. "Don't worry. I staged the whole thing. Now I want you to write about what you saw in the past few minutes. Immediately! Start now. As much detail as you can remember."

Still traumatized, we started to write. After about ten minutes, Father McGrath told us to stop.

The results of this experiment were most interesting. Everybody had a different memory of the event. Father McGrath had been stabbed in the stomach. Father McGrath had been stabbed in the back. Father McGrath's throat had been slit. Father McGrath had not been attacked at all. A girl was thrown out the window. A girl jumped out the window. Somebody had climbed in through the window. Different people saw different things.

I learned more than one lesson in that first class at business school. The first was that you must never completely believe what you see; you must always look beyond the immediate to understand what's going on. Even more relevant to the Directions meeting, Father McGrath demonstrated that unless you are extreme and experiential in the way you communicate, you will not make an impression or have a lasting impact.

And so I started the Directions meeting with my own version of the Adivasis' invasion, I came on stage, looked at the three or four thousand people in the audience, and started to dance. I am not the world's greatest dancer. People gasped and laughed. I made a complete fool of myself. I made some funny comments. And then we settled down to two hours of very serious conversation. The event ended up being as memorable to the HCLT audience as the attack of the Adivasis had been to me.

The Directions meetings pushed both reverse accountability and trust a bit further. There we were, the senior leadership team, standing up in front of the entire company, taking all questions, opening ourselves to every comment. Just by being available and by being as transparent as we could be in our comments and answers, we built trust with the members of the audience.

We conducted more than twenty-five Directions meetings during August and September 2006. We still do Directions meetings every year, and everybody looks forward to them. People expect an event that is unique and unorthodox. And they know that I will be there to listen effectively and communicate honestly about what *their* needs are, not mine. And sometimes I dance.

The Pyramid Begins to Invert

As the Smart Service Desk, the open 360-degree survey, and the Directions events gained acceptance and came to be seen as standard practice throughout the organization, my fears about the possibility of regression subsided. It looked as if the fundamental structure of HCLT was beginning to change, that the pyramid—thanks to reverse accountability and open review—was beginning to invert, at least a little. Eventually, we might really see the value zone exalted and the former pharaohs standing in its shadow.

Once more, the specific tools we had used to create the inversion—just like the other EFCS initiatives I have described earlier—were nothing more than catalysts. Did they really have as much effect on the organization, in and of themselves, as they seemed to have? Probably not. The message they sent, and the secondary effects they had, mattered much more.

Yes, SSD resolves many issues and fixes many problems. But the underlying message it sends is far more significant: *the new accountabilities are not determined by one's position in the traditional hierarchy.*

The 360-degree survey helps people improve their performance and pushes trust and transparency. The message it sends is much bigger: *a manager's value is measured by his or her span of influence, not by the zone of hierarchical control. That includes the CEO.*

These catalysts—along with the open financial information and U&I—changed the day-to-day conversations at HCLT. They communicated everything that needed to be shared about what employees were supposed to do and how they should engage.

Their fears about change began to dissipate, just as my fears about there being too little change faded away. People no longer looked at me with such trepidation and concern. They knew that the HCLT "crowd"—not I alone—would be evaluating them.

As a result, people stretched themselves more. They attempted more. Failure became acceptable. The responsibility for actions and results was not mine alone. It was shared by many. When I said that I, as CEO, was accountable for something, I knew that we are all accountable together. And the company knew it, too.

We also began to get indications that the outside world was noticing us and taking interest in what we were doing. In December 2006, I was invited by the CEO of one of our customers, a *Fortune* 100 company, to speak at its annual leadership conference. I had never met the CEO before I arrived for the meeting. When it came my turn to speak, he introduced me by saying that he had learned about our 360-degree survey from an HCLT employee who was working on a project that he was personally involved with. The survey intrigued him, and he wanted to learn more about it.

Four years later, that customer has become one of our largest and most important—a company whose CEO I had met through an employee who worked at the bottom of the HCLT pyramid. Since that first speaking engagement, I have been invited by many other customers to speak to their leadership teams and boards of directors about inverting the pyramid. Every one of those connections was made by an employee working in the value zone.

These introductions provided further proof that we were walking the right path. People stopped staring at the Himalayas and trying to guess what lay beyond. Instead, they looked at each other and knew that they could make anything happen.

CHAPTER FOUR

Recasting the Role of the CEO

Transferring the Responsibility for Change

By midwinter of 2006, people throughout HCLT had started to believe in the enormous potential we had as a company. They saw that our commitment to transparency and our efforts to invert the pyramid were making a tangible difference. We were now regularly and successfully competing with the best global players, just as we had vowed we would at our Blueprint meeting. This was satisfying to me, to the leadership team, and to employees throughout the company.

Yet, as I had with each previous phase of the process, I began to look ahead and worry. Just as we had intended, we were starting to speed up our growth. We were taking on hundreds of new people. Although we were still a relatively small company, at under $1 billion in annual worldwide revenue, we were quite diversified, with operations in eighteen countries in ten vertical areas, and with eight lines of service.

As we grew, how could we sustain our focus on Employees First, Customers Second? Wouldn't individual units start to rebuild their own traditional pyramid? Wouldn't new layers of management seek to gain power by aggregating information? How would new people coming on board understand the importance of trust and transparency?

Around that time, I was reading *The Starfish and the Spider: The Unstoppable Power of Leaderless Organizations*, by Ori Brafman and Rod A. Beckstrom.[1] Most companies, they argue, function like eight-legged spiders. "Cut off the leg of a spider, and you have a seven-legged creature on your hands; cut off its head and you have a dead spider," Beckstrom writes on his Web site. "But cut off the arm of a starfish and it will grow a new one. Not only that, but the severed arm can grow an entirely new body. Starfish can achieve this feat because, unlike spiders, they are decentralized; every major organ is replicated across each arm."

At that time, HCLT operated more like a spider than a starfish. For all our openness and transparency, and for all of our inverting of the pyramid, we were still a highly centralized organization. The CEO and, just as important, the office of the CEO, still stood at the center of every-thing, just like the head of the spider.

I saw that we needed to become more like the starfish and that this would require us to rethink the role of the CEO and to transfer much more of the responsibility for change to the employees. Only in that way could we continue to focus on the value zone, put employees first as our company continued to gain in size and scope, and make the change truly sustainable.

I began to look for ways that we could accelerate the transfer.

A Revelation

One day during the winter of 2006 I caught my first glimpse of what the starfish HCLT might look like. The CIO of a global customer was visiting our offices in Delhi to meet with his technical team. I made a point of stop-ping by to say hello a few minutes before the meeting got started.

"How is everything going?" I asked the CIO, who was working on his laptop in the conference room where the meeting would be held.

"Very well," he said. "The team is handling everything to our satisfaction."

"Fantastic," I said. "Then, if we don't need to discuss your current project, I'd like to tell you about a new service approach we're working on."

"Of course," the CIO said. "Please."

"It's called Business-Aligned IT, or BAIT," I said. "The goal is to much more closely align our services with our customers' specific business processes. We're working on a pilot right now, and we plan to roll out the full program to all our customers in the next few months."

"I know all about BAIT," the CIO said.

"What?" I said. I was taken aback. "How could you know about it? It's an internal pilot. Only a couple of customers and a few employees know about it."

"Your people told me about it. My HCLT team. How else could I know?"

"But we haven't even rolled this out internally. Your team hasn't been through the training yet," I said.

"Well, not only does the team know about BAIT, they've already put it to work for us. They identified our three most critical business processes. Analyzed them. Determined how to align them with HCLT solutions. And estimated the amount of money we can save over a twelve-month, twenty-four-month, and thirty-six-month period."

I did not know how to react. I was a little concerned that the team was using the BAIT process before it had been formally introduced throughout the company. On the other hand, I saw this as an example of the responsibility for change being transferred, without *any* involvement from me or the office of the CEO. It was happening organically.

At that moment, the team entered the room, ready for its scheduled meeting.

"I have just been telling Vineet about our work with the BAIT process," the CIO said to Tarika, the team leader. She looked a little abashed, not sure how I would react.

"Yes," I said. "And I am very interested to learn more about it."

Tarika (name changed) went to the whiteboard and grabbed a marker. Over the next ten minutes, she and her colleagues, with occasional interjections from the CIO, sketched out flow charts of the customer's three business processes, described the solutions in detail, and went through the cost savings analysis. I could not help but be infected by their enthusiasm and excitement.

What Tarika and her team had accomplished was pretty amazing, considering that our BAIT framework was not an official offering for us yet and, even more important, that these people were engineers, not business analysts. Their skills lay in implementing technology solutions, and they had little experience in dissecting strategic business processes and reducing cycle times. The last time I had checked in with the team, they had been working on a very straightforward application development.

When they finished their impromptu presentation, I asked, "So tell me how you made the shift from a technology solution to thinking more broadly about business strategy."

Tarika told me that she had heard about the BAIT pilot through one of her colleagues in a different area of the company. He had described it to her, and she thought it could be very helpful to the CIO's company. However, the HCLT consultants who were expert at BAIT were all too busy with the pilot project to help Tarika and her team. And besides, she knew that the customer didn't have any extra budget to pay for a consultant.

"So," Tarika explained, "I said to the team, 'Let's see if we can learn this on our own.' And everybody agreed to try." Over the next three months, in off moments and after regular business hours, the team members educated themselves and gained a much better understanding of the use of IT in driving change in core business processes. Once they thought they had sufficient knowledge, they asked an HCLT business consultant to do a workshop for them so that they could learn more about how to use the BAIT methods and tools.

"Then we applied the framework to the information we had gathered about our customer's business processes," Tarika said, "and made our recommendations in a business transformation report." She held up a thick document. "In it we describe what changes we would implement and how they could save several millions of dollars each year."

I shook my head. "This is fantastic work," I replied. "Especially since you have done it on your own time with almost no help from the formal organization or your managers."

Tarika and the team members smiled and tried to look as if it were no big deal.

When I left the office that day, I kept thinking about Tarika and her technical team. They had made a fundamental shift in the way they worked and how they added value for the customer without being directed to do so by me or any superior. The responsibility for change had been transferred, almost unconsciously, because of all of the efforts that had come before.

I thought: this is how EFCS can become adaptable and sustainable as HCLT grows. Men and women, like the members of this technical team, will take on the responsibility for change. They will see the CEO differently, not as the source of all change but as a kind of stimulator and enabler of change.

How could I recast the role of the CEO to make that clear to the entire organization and to accelerate the transfer of responsibility for change to HCLT employees around the world?

Reversing the Transfer of Responsibility: A New Dimension of the U&I Portal

Around that time, I was attending a number of seminars, including the World Economic Forum and *Fortune* magazine's BrainstormTECH conference in San Francisco, where I talked about the EFCS concept. At these events, I always got the same "yes, but" question.

"Mr. Nayar," someone would say, "this is all very interesting. But aren't many of these Employees First initiatives closely linked to your personal tenure in the job? How many of them do you think will produce long-term change? Won't they all fall apart after you have moved on?"

It was a good and valid question, and it nagged at me now. Every new CEO comes in with his or her initiatives. The organization takes the programs on board as much or as little as it can. When the next CEO arrives, months or years later, many of those initiatives are swept away and new ones put in their place. Too often, the CEO's initiatives create shifts in the organization that are not sustainable and do not produce *everlasting* change—that is, deep-down, fundamental, long-term change.

A possible solution showed up in an unexpected place: my e-mail box. During the winter of 2006, I was receiving a huge volume of e-mail every day. Even with all the initiatives we had put in place to increase transparency, to build trust, and to invert the organizational pyramid, a large percentage of the messages were still of the "Vineet, please tell me the answer to my question" kind. They would describe a problem or an issue and then conclude with a question like, "What do you recommend?" or "What should we do?" or "How should we handle this one?"

The people who sent them were, in effect, putting the responsibility for change on me, my office, or someone I might refer the problem to. But our aim was to transfer responsibility to the employees, not take it off their shoulders. It was not that the people sending the questions couldn't answer the questions for themselves. Many of the e-mailers were brighter than I was, after all, and knew a lot more about the particular technology, product, or geography they were asking about than I did or ever could. More important, they were closer to the value zone and had a better understanding of what should be done to create more value for the company and its customers. So why did they continue to look to me for solutions? They knew I couldn't have the answers to all their questions. I *shouldn't* have the answers in an organization with the multiple lines of service, markets, and operations that we did. There were so many value zones at such a distance from me, and we had a hugely diverse set of issues and problems.

I realized that employees were asking me such questions for two reasons. First, it was simply a habit, an unthinking response, typical of any command-and-control organization in which employees automatically look upward for answers. Second, perhaps they didn't want to take complete responsibility for the answer or for the outcome. They wanted me—the CEO—and my office to take some or all of the responsibility. Perhaps they wanted to be able to say, "Well, Vineet said it was OK. Don't blame me." Very possibly, I *was* to blame. Maybe I had led them to believe that I *did* want to make all the decisions, and thus perhaps I was the cause of their behavior.

Whatever the reason, this situation had to change. Employees had to take much more responsibility for their ideas and actions. After I discussed the issue at length with the leadership team and many colleagues, we hit on a simple catalyst for recasting the role of the CEO: add a new function to the U&I portal.

Our original goal with U&I had been to create transparency and thus build trust. We had succeeded in doing those things. But now I saw that in our desire to be transparent and make the CEO accessible and open, we had actually enhanced the perception of the all-knowing CEO and his all-powerful office; we had unintentionally reinforced the idea that the CEO would take responsibility for everything. The premise of U&I, after all, was that anyone could send Vineet a question, and that I, or some member of my office, would quickly get back to the questioner with an answer.

This quest for transparency had served to centralize power in the office of the CEO even more than before. But, as I had learned in that client meeting with Tarika and her technical team, much more knowledge existed outside my office than within it. It dawned on me that *I* had a lot of questions to ask of others. "Vineet," I said to myself, "you are an employee, too, after all." Why shouldn't this question asking go both ways? I was struggling with a lot of issues at the time, many of which I simply could not solve by myself. Rather than hide my struggles or pretend I had the answers, why not seek help from the organization? Wouldn't that take a chip out of the marble facade of the office of the CEO?

So, we created a new section within U&I called My Problems. It was about just that: *my* problems, the questions that I, as CEO, could not answer or solve myself. I started posting questions that I was struggling with, and people began to send me answers. One issue, in particular, was galling me. As you may know, there is a group of analyst companies that have a lot of clout in the IT buyer community. These very smart organizations conduct research, offer consulting to clients, and have a significant influence on how IT customers think. They are intermediaries in the market, often standing between service companies and customer companies.

At that time, some of these intermediaries seemed to have a strong bias toward the global IT suppliers, which we were now competing against so successfully. Some of these analysts, though few in number, seemed to believe that big was always better and, accordingly, would recommend that their clients always go for size even when smaller players like HCLT could demonstrate a better value proposition. This frustrated me because I knew that we had just as much capacity and capability as, if not more than, the global players did to create value for our customers, and that we had greater ability to innovate and come up with disruptive changes. In other words, it was far more likely that we would be the Apple or Google of the IT industry, rather than those that were considered a safer bet. But some of the analysts seemed unable to hear that message or, if they heard it, to believe in it. Perhaps it was because we had not adequately communicated our message and proved our claims about ourselves.

One of the first posts I wrote in the My Problems section of U&I was about this issue. "How should we reach out to analysts to change their views? What proofs can we give them about our new capabilities and our unique approach?" I asked. And I followed that one up with a few other conundrums I could not crack.

I got an incredibly large number of responses. It was as if everyone in the organization had an opinion on the topic and was only too willing to help out their poor, benighted CEO. Were all the organizational problems solved by the answers I got through My Problems? Did I get perfect, ready-to-implement solutions to my every concern? No, of course not. But we heard many interesting points, ideas, and suggested remedies that helped me understand the problem better and develop my thinking. In many cases, I engaged in a back-and-forth with the contributors, as we asked each other questions such as:

- What is the fundamental nature of the problem?

- How does it really affect us?

- Do we really need to do something about it?

- Who is the right person or team to think more about this?

- What timeline makes sense?

- How will we evaluate the process and the solution?

This conversation, by focusing on "my problems and your answers," started to shift the responsibility of actions that could create change away from me to other people throughout the organization. It became a dialogue rather than a monologue.

Then we took the concept a step further and posted policy ideas we were thinking about and solicited comment from employees. We created opinion polls about various issues and showed the results for all to see. The leadership team did not always accept the advice that we received, nor did we always follow the majority opinion expressed in the polls. That was not the real purpose of this idea. The goal was to get the whole company talking and listening to one another, just like a good family, and for the management to justify and communicate their decisions when they were at variance with majority views.

It was another step toward recasting the role of the office of the CEO. If the CEO was not willing or able to answer all the employees' questions, and if he actually asked them for answers to the problems he was wrestling with, weren't we redistributing responsibility for our fates, sharing it? Didn't that mean that everyone in the company had to take responsibility for creating value in the value zone? Wouldn't this ensure that our competitive advantage would remain beyond any CEO's tenure? Didn't that mean that we all had to take responsibility and spread the philosophy of EFCS to new employees so that it would carry on?

Engaging the Whole Person

But we had to do still more to encourage people to take on greater responsibility for change within the company. Not everyone communicated with me through U&I, after all, either by asking his or her own questions or trying to answer mine. And there were still plenty of employees who simply did not engage completely with the company. Their job was just a job; what they really cared about lay outside the work environment and beyond the workday.

Around that time, I had a fascinating conversation with the CIO of an important global 100 company. We had just won a contract with him to greatly expand our scope of engagement with his company. After the deal was done, I asked the CIO why he had selected HCLT over the other vendors that had bid for the business.

It was a pro forma question, to which, at first, he gave a pro forma answer. He talked about the innovativeness of our solutions, the quality of our service, our responsiveness, our facilities and locations, and our pricing. But then he said, "However, Vineet, I really think that the entire bidding process for jobs like this makes very little sense. We put out a request for a proposal, and you diligently respond to it. But it doesn't really tell us what we want to know about you or your company."

"What do you mean?" I asked. "Are you saying that our proposal was inadequate?"

"Not at all," he said. "After all, we chose you. What I'm saying is that the proposal did not address the really important issues."

"Such as?"

"Such as what your people are all about. Who are they? What do they think about? What are their ethics? What are they passionate about? I don't need to know about the tools and technologies they're going to use. They will be very similar to the ones that people in every other company use. I want to know if they will walk the extra mile for me and my project. Will they get excited enough to share their knowledge beyond what's in the contract? Will they engage their whole selves in their work with us?"

This idea struck me deeply. If we could engage people around their passions and beliefs and ethics, wouldn't they be more likely to take responsibility for change? Wouldn't they demand it?

But how could we begin to understand the role of passion at work?

Identifying Sources of Passion: The EPIC Survey

Lots of companies conduct surveys that seek to measure employee satisfaction or employee engagement. But as I thought about the CIO's remarks, I realized that these approaches were inadequate. Is satisfaction really a useful indication of anything? Satisfaction is very different from passion. Doesn't satisfaction actually imply a complacent acceptance of how things already are? If I am satisfied, will I be interested in changing or improving anything?

And what about engagement? Is that any better? I suppose that if an employee is engaged, that is better than being disengaged. But isn't it just another, slightly more active form of satisfaction? I am engaged with the work and the project, but does that mean I am asking questions about it? Have I considered better ways? Will I walk the extra mile that my CIO friend so highly valued?

Probably not. Only passion makes people jump out of bed in the morning looking forward to the work of the day. Only passion pushes them to try things that may be difficult or seem impossible. Only passion makes them take on responsibilities or accept tasks that are not strictly specified in a contract document.

So, we asked ourselves, how can we measure and tap into an employee's passion? How could we improve our understanding of what he or she really loves and wants to do? Could we use such a measure to help people find and

follow their passions and therefore become more passionate toward their jobs?

We didn't know, but we decided to try.

To that end, we developed an initiative called the
Employee Passion Indicative Count (EPIC).

We identified a short list of the main drivers of passion and organized them into three themes: self, social,
and secular. We created a survey, with questions organized
into those three themes. The goal of the survey was to
identify the core values that are of most importance to
people and that drive their potential to act passionately,
both personally and professionally.

The passion survey turned out to be a huge hit. People
loved thinking about the passion they had, or did not have,
for the jobs they were doing. They were intrigued to learn
what others were doing to drive passion in their respective
areas. Managers were able to take the pulse of their employees in a different way. Interest in the survey spawned several
post-EPIC workshops and team interventions, all of which
helped people think more about their passion indicators
and how they could best leverage them at work.

Creating Sustainable Communities of Passion: The Employee First Councils

Next, we needed a way to embed people's passion into the
organizational structure. We struck upon the idea of creating employee communities that would be called *Employee*

First Councils and would be organized around a specific area of passion, much like a college club. The councils would be virtual, spanning all organizational boundaries, but would have an elected representative in each physical facility.

The idea caught on like wildfire. Councils were created around health and hygiene, art, music, corporate social responsibility, and dozens of other issues. Today, some twenty-five hundred people serve as council leaders around the world and have a team of council members across geographies who participate according to their areas of interest or passion. It's a democratic exercise; the leaders are elected by the employees, rather than appointed by management. This practice further pushes control away from the office of the CEO and out into the arms of the starfish.

The effect of these councils has been amazing. They allow people to enhance their persona at work. Employees become so engaged in these groups that the councils have provided a new way to spread learning throughout the organization and bring the whole person, as well as the person's families, into the culture of the company.

Employee First Councils proved so popular and so powerful in energizing our people, in fact, that we began to think about how the groups could be put to work to affect our business more directly. To that end, we added communities that focused specifically on business-related passions such as a particular technology or a vertical domain area. Soon enough, these business-focused communities were generating all kinds of ideas for HCLT, helping us to develop plans and come up with proposals for new business. (The idea for BAIT, for example, originated in one such business-focused community.) When some of these ideas began to produce new revenue, we realized that we had stumbled on another unanticipated benefit: creating new business ideas through unstructured innovation.

One such complex unstructured innovation, centered around cloud computing, is in progress at HCLT as I write this book. Organizations around the world are trying to improve their understanding of cloud computing, which essentially moves applications off the desktop and company servers and onto the Web, as it is sure to have a far-reaching impact on IT suppliers and their customers. Business models will undergo radical change; some will not survive. No single person, team, or community owns the issue of cloud computing at HCLT, because its implications are immense for all our lines of business.

But the debate and community participation help us increase awareness, create a sense of urgency, encourage new thought, and prevent us from being blindsided by change. As CEO, I am just one of many voices in the conversation. As a result, our strategic response to cloud computing is constantly evolving. When a specific approach gains critical mass within the council, it is transferred to a group that focuses on execution. It is my belief that innovation, especially in our business, often thrives in an unstructured process like this one.

These communities of passion—built around personal interests and business issues—had the desired effect on the structure of the company. They helped to further transfer the responsibility of new-idea generation beyond the office of the CEO and the leadership team and into communities of people collaborating and creating alternatives outside the boundaries of hierarchy.

Gradually, step by step, catalyst by catalyst, the office of the CEO was becoming a little less like the all-knowing spider's head. The company was becoming a bit more like the starfish.

Transferring Responsibility for Setting Strategy

Since beginning our efforts at recasting the role of the CEO in 2006 and transferring responsibility for change to our employees, we have pursued many other catalysts and initiatives. For example, we began to see that we had to change the relationship with our customers and enable them to take more responsibility for where our partnerships and new endeavors were headed. We already had a customer advisory group and a quarterly steering committee meeting focused on customer issues, but we wanted to involve the customer more deeply in creating value and, at the same time, to further challenge our employees to take more responsibility beyond their defined roles.

Soon enough, we had a proposed solution: create an idea exchange, to be called a *value portal*, between the customer and our employees. Employees could generate and register new value-creating ideas, then share them with customers, who would evaluate and rate the ideas on various specific criteria. For participating and generating well-rated ideas, the employees would be recognized and rewarded.

Within a short time after we implemented the value portal, more than a hundred customers had joined in. Meanwhile, HCLT employees had generated thousands of ideas with the potential of saving hundreds of millions of dollars for our customers.

Then we were ready for what might be seen as the ultimate step: enabling employees to share in the responsibility for the setting of our company's strategy, working together to determine our future.

I must jump ahead to 2009 to describe the most potent expression of this approach, a concept called *MyBlueprint*. As I described earlier, in 2005 we held our first Blueprint meeting, a gathering of our senior managers to talk about where we should be headed in the coming five years. In 2009, we were nearing the end of that plan and needed to map out the next leg of the journey.

About three hundred managers had responsibility for making plans for their specific business areas. In past years, their written plans and oral presentations had been reviewed by the next person up the hierarchical ladder, including me. In 2009, as we were recasting the role of the CEO, I found myself in the midst of the annual review process. I asked myself, Why should I be the one to review all of these? What do I know about the businesses of these three hundred managers? How can I really evaluate them? What value am I adding? Wouldn't it make more sense for a manager in financial services to hear views on how retail companies are innovating in building relationships with their end consumers, or how media and publishing companies are innovating in tracking and monetizing digital content—both of which could possibly trigger new ideas or solutions for this manager's financial services customer? Wouldn't a manager in Australia learn a lot from a peer in Europe who had faced similar issues and challenges?

So, in 2009, we decided not to hold a live Blueprint meeting at all.

Instead, we agreed that the three hundred managers would each prepare and record their plans, and the recordings would be posted on a MyBlueprint portal, rather like Facebook. The plans would be open for review by another eight thousand HCLT managers, including people above the managers in the traditional hierarchy and those below them. This, we hoped, would transform the planning process into a peer-to-peer review rather than a top-down judgment. It would bring planning much closer to the value zone. It would further shift responsibility away from the office of the CEO.

Did the "yes, buts" fly?

Of course they did.

"But, Vineet, that means *you* won't look at the plans?"

"You want us to share our plans with eight thousand managers? That's pushing transparency much too far. We'll give away our strategy. The whole world will find out where we're headed!"

"Vineet, we have always prepared these for executive eyes only. What form should they take in a MyBlueprint portal?"

We went forward anyway. And the effect has been astonishing. The three hundred managers posted their plans. When I listened to a few of the recordings, I was surprised to find that they sounded very different from the face-to-face presentations I had heard over the previous four years. Because the managers knew that the recordings would be reviewed by a large number of people, including their own teams, the depth of their business analysis and the quality of their planned strategy improved. They were more honest in their assessment of current challenges and opportunities. They talked less about what they hoped to accomplish and more about the actions they intended to take to achieve specific results.

As always, the catalyst had unanticipated secondary effects. Eight thousand HCLT managers took advantage of the opportunity to review the recordings on the MyBlueprint portal. Soon enough, the network was buzzing. People pointed their colleagues to a recording they thought would be useful. Employees within a department discussed their futures with new understanding, and they loved the transparency. The amount of knowledge sharing outside the walls of the formal hierarchy was extraordinary. Managers made new connections with one another across all kinds of boundaries.

People posted comments about the strategies that provided the managers with new perspectives and ideas that were far more relevant and actionable than the inputs managers had typically received in their annual reviews. When a new employee joined the team, he or she had a place to go to learn what the team was trying to achieve and why. Everyone felt able to contribute to the thinking and planning process. People understood the challenges better, owned the plan, and could align themselves with the strategy as I had never seen before.

In the end, the leadership team and I participated in the process, giving comment and feedback, but our voices were just a few among the eight thousand.

Was the MyBlueprint process a success? I think so. Will we do it the same way again next year? Probably, but there will undoubtedly be new twists and turns, new refinements and new catalysts. Nothing is ever perfect.

Pushing Responsibility to an Acquired Company: The Reverse Merger of AXON

Our efforts to share responsibility with employees and units of the company extended to the way we handled mergers and acquisitions, as well. In December 2008, HCLT completed the acquisition of a U.K.-based SAP consultancy firm, AXON Plc, for £440 million, the largest overseas acquisition by an Indian IT company to date.

At the time, SAP business management software was growing fast. We were not able to organically create high-end SAP consulting capabilities. AXON was the largest and most successful independent SAP consulting company in the world, so we acquired the company to help us strengthen our offering and grow faster.

We were determined, however, not to make the mistake that so many companies make with their acquisitions: forcing the AXON organization to integrate into the HCLT organization. Instead, we recognized that we had acquired AXON because we were weak in this space and it was strong, and thus we should be in the business of enabling AXON to succeed rather than focusing on how to integrate it into HCLT. Accordingly, we merged our SAP organization, of some twenty-five hundred people, into AXON. Then, we enabled HCL AXON to be even more successful by allowing it to leverage HCLT'S balance sheet, brand, reach, customers, solutions, and innovation framework. The approach worked so well that nine months after the acquisition, the HCL AXON leadership team took charge of running many other parts of HCLT businesses.

Thus, HCL AXON and the rest of HCLT achieved a good deal of growth, HCLT's customers could take advantage of a new value proposition, and our stock price rose, even during the downturn of 2008–2009. And as CEO, I gained bandwidth to do more and more. Or perhaps I should say, to do less and less. In other words, much of the responsibility that would typically have been transferred to the office of the CEO in an acquisition actually went in the opposite direction.

We saw that the EFCS concept, when applied to a large acquisition like the AXON merger, could generate such powerful results that we completed four more successful acquisitions in that year. With each of them, we proved that when a CEO focuses less on governing and more on enabling, the executive can accomplish much that might otherwise have been too risky to undertake.

The Benefits of Transferring Responsibility for Change

Many people have questioned me about this recasting of the role of the CEO. Am I really serious about it? Mustn't the CEO hold tight to the reins of power? How can a company set strategy in a collaborative process?

I deeply believe that a good deal of responsibility for managing the company must be transferred to employees, for three reasons:

- First, concentrating power in the office of the CEO drains power away from the value zone.

The office of the CEO is always too far away from the value zone to really understand the zone. The CEO who tries to drive what happens there, especially in services and knowledge economy companies, may simply drive it into the ground.

- The second reason is speed. The speed of thought, of change, and of implementation gets suffocated by too much hierarchy, wherever it may be. The only way to remove hierarchy in the organization is to recast the role of the CEO as one who asks more questions than he or she answers. The rest of the hierarchy will soon tumble.

- The third reason to recast the role of the office of the CEO is the element of knowledge. The complexity of the knowledge and service economies is so great that it is impossible for any individual or company unit, including the CEO and the office of the CEO, to possess all the knowledge. The CEO must be in the business of enabling the people who *do* have the knowledge to do what they are good at, rather than taking decisions on his or her own, using incomplete, imperfect, and probably outdated knowledge.

The CEO can no longer be the one who scribbles strategy on a paper napkin over dinner. He or she cannot be the one who stands in front of a crowd to motivate it with fabulous oratory. The CEO will not be the one who thinks of the best and the brightest ideas. The role of the CEO is to enable people to excel, help them discover their own wisdom, engage themselves entirely in their work, and accept responsibility for making change.

Toward Self-Direction

I have a very personal and long-standing argument with hierarchy. Perhaps that is why I am so intent on rethinking the role of the CEO and getting others to share the responsibility for the work of the company.

I was fortunate that the teachers in my school operated in the role of enablers of learning. They wanted to transfer the control of our education to the students, as early in our lives as possible. They did not think of themselves as CEOs of the classroom.

In our family, there wasn't much hierarchy either. My father died young, when I was a teenager. So the traditional command-and-control structure that he might have followed simply did not exist in our household.

Over the years, I have watched and studied other institutions, from philanthropic organizations to religious groups, searching for clues and models that might be applied to business. I have concluded that when people feel passion and responsibility for what they do, not only can they transform a company, they can also transform themselves.

Once we transfer the ownership of our collective problems from the supposedly all-powerful CEO to the employees, people want to transform and deal with their professional and personal lives in a very different way than they ever did before. Suddenly, they see the company as their own enterprise. They start thinking like entrepreneurs. Their energy quotient leaps up. And when that happens with a critical mass of employees (usually, 5 or 10 percent is all you need) throughout the company, it creates a kind of fusion—a coming together of the human particles in the corporate molecule that releases a massive amount of energy.

So, the ultimate goal of all of the initiatives I have described in this chapter goes beyond the recasting of the role of the CEO; it is the creation of a self-governing, self-organizing company. We are not there yet at HCLT. Give us a few more droplets and a little more time.

Many managers within our organization have become flag wavers for our efforts to shift responsibility for change away from the office of the CEO and for the quest toward self-governance. "But it's not always the easiest way to get things done," they have often admitted to me. "Then again, the easiest way usually isn't as much fun."

Indeed, I have seen people flounder as they struggle to make decisions and take responsibility for themselves and for their organizational units. I myself have stumbled many times. We have seen as many failures as we have successes. At many forums, I have debated the issues that surround the transference of responsibility to employees as well as the entire EFCS concept. Sometimes I have been unable to do full justice to our ideas and have probably failed to convince some of those who were engaged in the conversation.

Nonetheless, we have continued to successfully walk the path of Employees First, Customers Second. What has made it possible, and what has personally given me the strength to continue, is the faith and passion of employees throughout the HCLT organization—those people who are the essential droplets of change—who put so much of their minds and hearts into our company and its transformation.

Without them, we would long ago have slid down the hillside and found ourselves looking up at a mountain too high for us to climb.

CHAPTER FIVE

Find Understanding in Misunderstanding

Renewing the Cycle of Change

Perhaps it is easier to misunderstand the Employees First, Customers Second concept than it is to understand it. There are many ways to *not* see it for what it is.

So, in this final chapter, I want to talk more about what EFCS really is and what it isn't; what it can do for you, your company, and your employees; and what it cannot do. This is, perhaps, an inversion of how you might expect a book like this to be structured (but, after all, the main theme of the book is about the value of inverting traditional structures, so we might as well turn this one upside down too!), because in the preceding chapters I have talked about the practical issues and specific steps we took on our journey. Now I want to address the misunderstandings related to this philosophy.

The First Misunderstanding: It Won't Work When Times Get Tough

"Yes, Mr. Nayar, this is all very well and good," I can hear people saying to me. "Your stories about mirrors and droplets of rain and poultry farms are interesting and some-times even inspiring. But what happens when times get tough? What happens when your company hits a bad patch? When the economy goes sour? When your whole industry becomes irrelevant?"

"Above all, Mr. Nayar, what happens when you have no choice but to cut costs and, God forbid, reduce the head count of your precious employees? Will they still think you're accountable to them when you hand them the pink slip?"

Funny you should ask.

We at HCLT faced the same problems that most com-panies did during the worst of the economic crisis—most fundamentally, a serious threat of decline in business. During that period, from the middle of 2008 to the end of 2009, the Employees First, Customers Second concept was truly put to the test. We asked ourselves, is this concept relevant at a time like this? Can we afford to put our employees first when our customers themselves are struggling? Won't we have to have layoffs? Isn't that the only way to keep costs low in a time when the top line is suffering? And won't that go against the whole Employees First idea?

I talked it over with my leadership team. We didn't really know how to respond to the threat of declining business in a severe economic crisis, because we had never had to deal with such a situation. We refused, however, to believe that a wholesale layoff of employees was the only answer to reducing costs and surviving the downturn. We felt in our hearts that if we refused to see the recession as an excuse for declining performance, and if we did the right thing for our employees, then we could convert the threat into an opportunity.

This conviction was supported by my belief that the entire knowledge economy is built on the trust that employees and their employers have in each other; there really is nothing else. It is only this relationship—the one between employees and the organization—that keeps a company going. If you do a large-scale layoff that is not related to the employees' performance, but is solely about cost-cutting, the fabric of trust is torn. The premise on which the organization exists is negated.

We had to find a different, no-excuse way. So we stuck to our Employees First principles and took the route of transparency, reverse accountability, and collective wisdom. We reached out to ten thousand HCLT employees, through live events and online media, and said, "How should we respond to this challenge? Give us your thoughts and ideas." We called the program *Smart Response*.

As we had come to expect, the response was immediate and massive. And, as we learned from earlier initiatives, not all the ideas were useful. We did, however, end up with fifteen initiatives that we implemented and that resulted in huge cost savings for the company. Although the initiatives, as implemented, looked quite different from the original suggestions we received through Smart Response, that is not the point. The senior management team and I never could have conceptualized these initiatives on our own. We improvised on them, refined them, took them further, and ended up with a very strong list of finalists.

Surprisingly, the suggestions included ideas about reducing the size of the workforce by asking people who were performing below standard, or who were not flexible, to leave the company. The employees who made the suggestions argued that we had to weed out the free riders in order to survive and, very important, to motivate the high performers.

The ultimate impact of the Smart Response initiative was less on cost-cutting initiatives than it was on increasing revenues. When our employees were engaged to find an answer to the tough question of how best to weather the recession, they felt included and assured about their future, and started to focus on how to create more excitement in the customer interface so as to increase share of wallet. This was very different from the situation in some other IT companies, many of which had not adopted an inclusive approach for considering responses to the recession. Employees in such companies were uncertain and focused on their own fates, and they felt demotivated and afraid. It showed in their performance in the value zone and compounded the problems for their companies, which created a doom spiral of worsening performance and deepening anxiety. While market share of those companies dropped, HCLT grew 20 percent year after year during the worst period of the recession. We closed orders worth twice as much as in the same period the previous year, and we made thousands of new job offers across the globe during those months. In the United States and the United Kingdom we added fifteen hundred employees.

Management expert Gary Hamel pointed out the wisdom of this approach well before the recession hit. He wrote: "Unfortunately, a threat that everyone perceives but no one talks about creates more anxiety than a threat that has been clearly identified and made the focal point for the problem-solving efforts of the entire company."[1]

I asked several of our large customers why they thought we had been able to improve our market share during that time. They all said the same thing: "Your employees made the magic happen."

The set of ideas that resulted from the Smart Response process enabled HCLT to manage the slowdown better than many of our competitors, and even more important, it proved that the EFCS concept does work in tough times. Did we get everything right? Probably not, but the Smart Response catalyst was sufficient to bring about a significant change in employee behavior and create the desired business result.

The Second Misunderstanding: We Don't Need It, Because Times Are Good

Strangely enough, I also get this inverse reaction to Employees First: not only will it fail to work in tough times, but also that it is unnecessary in good times. I counter that misconception with the story of the ant and the butterfly, a story demonstrating that breakthrough initiatives like EFCS are most needed when times are good, or seem to be good.

Consider the young ant. It learns from its father and mother and goes to college and then business school and earns its MBA. Somewhere along the way, the ant becomes quite impressed with itself. "I am a better ant than any other ant," it says. The ant that tries particularly hard can become an even better ant than it was before. And if it tries extra hard, it can become what I call a fast-walking ant. And, yes, if that ant gets some lucky breaks—like a big inheritance or a very fine spouse—it may become the fastest-walking ant of all.

However, it is still an ant.

Now, if you are an ant and wish to become a butterfly, that is a whole different matter. You must have tremendous desire to do so. You must be willing to give up all the things you liked about being an ant. You must accept that all the knowledge you had about how to be the fastest-walking ant won't help you become a butterfly. You will need a different kind of knowledge altogether.

Look at the evolution of Mohan Das Karamchand Gandhi into Mahatma Gandhi. How did he do it? He came up with an idea—nonviolence—that had not been considered before, that was not established, and that no other leaders were employing. He departed from the conventional, well-traveled paths and, instead, took an unconventional route. This road led him to an amazing place, somewhere that he—and his followers, his nation, and the world—had never been before.

An ant may become a CEO. But that ant will not become a true leader without transforming into a butterfly. The same holds true for human beings. If you are a traditional CEO, the only way to become a leader is to listen to your inner self. If it tells you to do something, and if you are able to do it, you may become the leader you wish to be.

I was reminded of this story when I attended a conference of CEOs on the West Coast in 2008. I spoke about EFCS there, and when the session was over and I was getting ready to leave, a young man, probably in his late thirties, approached me. He introduced himself as Huang Li (I have changed his name) and said that he was the CEO of a Chinese hotel chain. Huang started the conversation by complimenting me on my speech, but quickly followed up with a criticism that has become extremely familiar to me.

"Even though your ideas are very interesting to hear about, Mr. Nayar," he said with cold confidence, "I cannot imagine they are applicable to all situations."

I had heard this comment many times before and have heard it many times since. I smiled and invited Huang to join me for coffee in the Networking Lounge. As we sipped our lattes, we picked up the discussion.

"I have to say honestly," Huang began, "that I see no sense in the Employees First philosophy. At least not for me and my company."

I decided not to counter his arguments. Instead I asked him to tell me about his hotel business. Huang was more than willing to tell his story, as most people are. It seems that it was a family-owned company, the leader in its high-end segment of hotels and resorts in the region around Shanghai. (I have also changed the location of his business.) The key to the CEO's office had been passed down from generation to generation. As far as I could tell, the senior leadership was a group of aunts, uncles, and cousins, all genetically sewn together into one happy, loyal boardroom.

As Huang talked about the company's leadership, its heritage, and its culture, I quickly understood why he did not, and probably could not, believe in EFCS. He had been born into a closely held, family-governed enterprise. The idea that these imperial corporate rulers should be accountable to their employees would indeed have been totally ridiculous to him. I could not blame him for thinking that way.

After he told me about the business, we returned to our original topic of discussion, and again Mr. Huang questioned the concept. "Do you still think we need reverse accountability and all your revolutionary ideas?" he asked, with just a bit of a scoff. "You can see that everything is going just fine inside our company."

I guessed that he would not be having coffee with me if he truly believed that everything was perfectly fine in his company, so I decided to take a different tack with him.

"Tell me, Mr. Huang, what is your company's revenue growth?" I asked.

"It's 22 percent year on year," he said proudly.

"That's very good, I suppose," I said and paused.

Huang looked slightly offended. "Very good, indeed," he said. "That's 5 percent higher than the industry average."

"No doubt," I said. "But why isn't it better? Why not 40 or 50 percent year on year?"

Mr. Huang looked at me as if he had no idea what I was talking about.

"Well," I said, "the hospitality industry in China—and especially Shanghai where you are headquartered—is the golden goose right now, isn't it?"

"Of course it is!" Huang said with obvious self-satisfaction.

"And you have just told me that your company is the leader in the premium segment. So, if you are the top company in a fast-growing industry in the best market in the world, why are you clocking just 22 percent year-on-year growth?" I asked. "Especially when that's only 5 percent better than the average?"

Huang smirked at me, but I could see a tiny cloud of doubt in his eyes.

"I think the fact that your company is growing at only 22 percent year on year should actually be a cause for concern for you," I said.

"That's absurd," Huang said.

"Possibly so. Now, I assume that your hotels have the highest standards and all the best amenities and that your customers are serviced in the best possible way."

Huang nodded, not quite sure what I was getting at. "Yes, of course, everything is of the highest order," he assured me.

"And so how will you improve your growth rate next year and the year after that? Especially if the market cools down. Or your competitors match your standards?"

Mr. Huang fiddled with his coffee cup but did not reply.

"You asked me why you should reverse the accountability in your company and put employees first. My answer is that it is the only way for you to keep growing. That's the only way to improve your performance."

Huang was listening more attentively now.

"I am sure you have done everything you can to improve your tangible assets," I said. "Properties and amenities. Now I believe you must focus on your human capital.

To make a big leap ahead, especially when you're already performing at a high level, you have to put your employees first. You must do everything you can to enable them and be accountable to them. If you do, you will see your company exceed your own expectations as well as those of your customer. You will not have to settle for 22 percent growth. You may even achieve 40! Even more important, you will create a sustainable legacy and be long remembered for your success."

Huang laughed this time, and I laughed with him. But, when we took our leave of each other, I could see that Huang felt some discomfort. I had planted the seed of an idea in his mind. I hope that it found some sunlight and some nice rain droplets.

I had no doubt that Mr. Huang was a fast-walking ant, perhaps the fastest-walking ant in the Chinese hotel business. But I was not sure he could become a butterfly. Next time I'm in China, I will stay at one of Mr. Huang's hotels and find out.

The Third Misunderstanding: Customers Will Never See the Value

Now comes the third objection, which is that although the employees of an EFCS company may find value in the initiative, it is a delusion that customers will actually receive any direct value from it.

My answer to that misunderstanding is this: not only does the customer see the value very clearly, but the customer often sees it before we, the leadership, see it ourselves. Remember the stories about how customers perceived the employees as the real doers in our company and regarded me, and management in general, as a barrier or not important to their success?

It does little good for me to claim that customers see the value of the EFCS initiative. They have to say it themselves and, fortunately for me, they often do. This happened most memorably at a Global 100 (a group of chief executive officers of some of the world's most significant companies) meeting held in New York and hosted by Jack Welch, former CEO of General Electric. After my presentation, Jack began grilling me about whether the EFCS concept could help companies in recession. I launched into a long answer that must not have sounded very convincing, because, after a few moments, a member of the audience raised his hand and called out. He was the CEO of one of our major customers, a *Fortune* 100 company.

He stood up. "Jack, I have seen HCLT transform itself though EFCS, and I can vouch as a customer that it works for us, too." Wow! I knew that the CEO was an important supporter of HCLT, but I had no idea that he would make such a public and positive statement of the value of Employees First.

That's not all. Many of our customers tell me they love us specifically because of our commitment to our employees, and what's more, these customers have followed our lead in this movement. They, too, are implementing EFCS approaches in their companies, in their own ways. They often come to talk with HCLT employees about how they are doing in their own companies, looking for honest assessment and feedback.

Our customer satisfaction scores, which had been high and on the rise, actually went up by 43 percent during the 2008–2009 recession. Customers do gain direct value from the EFCS program, and believe me, they know it.

The Fourth Misunderstanding: Implementation Requires Large-Scale Initiatives

At HCLT, we did not implement any large-scale technical or organizational initiatives to implement EFCS. We relied instead on small-scale catalysts, tweaks to our existing systems, rethinking of processes, and lots of communication.

We can see the similarly large impact of small-scale technical changes in many other situations. The cell phone, for example, is bringing new economic clout, profit, and productivity to thousands of fishermen on the Indian coast.

While they are still at sea, the fishermen can call several ports to find the best prices, playing the dealers against one another to drive up the price. Dealers don't like the new balance of power, of course, but they pay higher prices to the fishermen who work this particular stretch of coastline.

Similarly, simple access to the Internet has had a major impact on Indian farmers. Typically economically disadvantaged and often illiterate, rural Indian farmers have had limited access to information and education about improved farming techniques that could enhance their yield. Farmers rarely have ready access to quality materials, such as the best seeds, herbicides, and pesticides, or to critical information such as accurate weather forecasts, which could help them improve the quality of their crops. Such inefficiencies kept their costs high and profits low.

The e-Choupal project (*choupal* means "village square" or "gathering place" in Hindi) brings Internet centers to farming villages. Through these centers, farmers of soybeans, wheat, coffee, and other crops have easy access to real-time information over the Internet. By knowing the current prices for wholesale products, these farmers can negotiate better prices for themselves and thus realize the greatest profit from their crops.

The response to this misunderstanding: a solution need not be large scale, complex, or require a huge initiative to bring about a spectacular result.

The Fifth Misunderstanding: This Has Nothing to Do with Performance

Even when I respond to questions about the first four misunderstandings, people still doubt that an initiative like EFCS can actually lead to significant growth and profit.

The best response to this misunderstanding is a few facts that pertain to the first four years (2005–2009) of our transformation:

- Seventy percent of all major deals closed by HCLT were won against the Big Four global IT players.

- The number of our customers grew fivefold. By annual revenue, $1 million–plus customers doubled, $5–10 million customers quadrupled, and $20 million–plus customers grew fivefold.

- Employee attrition has fallen by almost 50 percent. That includes a significant decline in attrition of performers rated "outstanding," which demonstrates our increased ability to retain our most valuable human resources.

- We achieved a 70 percent increase in ESAT (employee satisfaction), according to an external, independent survey.

- Revenues tripled over a four-year period.

- Operating income also tripled.

And we achieved all this while we were having lots of fun and not trying to be something other than what we actually were!

Unfinished Agenda: Making Change a Way of Life

As we have seen, the journey of Employees First, Customers Second progressed through a sequence of phases. These stages were: looking in the mirror, creating trust through transparency, inverting the pyramid, and transferring the responsibility for change to all.

In truth, the phases, as we lived through them, were not so well defined as they may appear as you read about them. We often found ourselves having to repeat one of the steps. Sometimes the entire sequence would have to be played through for a specific initiative or in a particular area of the company.

So EFCS must be seen as a cycle of activity, a journey that begins over and over again. But although the journey ceaselessly starts and restarts, it never plays out exactly the same way twice. Each time, we come up with new catalysts and continue to push our boundaries more vigorously so that we can change the company still further.

This is essential because the world of business is changing in fundamental ways. We all experience rapidly evolving consumer needs, greater regulation, a leveling of the
competitive playing field, and the ever-changing nature
of risk and ethics. Almost all the business leaders I know
are navigating through the multiplicity of forces as never
before. As complex as the business environment has
become, however, I still believe that there is always a very
simple route to success: a droplet, a catalyst that sets the
process in motion.

However, I do not claim to understand everything
about this subject, and I cannot be sure that the process
will work in the same way, or as well, in all companies,
all situations, and all geographies, as it has for us. I know
that there are imperfections and inconsistencies in our
approach. And when we run up against one of these, we
must look in the mirror once more, make a correction,
and start walking again. The beauty, ultimately, is in the
experiments and the learning we gain from them.

Many people—both inside and outside HCLT—
misunderstand what we are doing. But many *do* understand the philosophy of Employees First, Customers Second (and the thinking behind it), are excited by it, and
have put the ideas to work for them in their professional
and personal lives.

Many employees, for example, have applied what they
have learned at HCLT in setting up and running their
own small social enterprises. Others teach our philosophy

at schools and colleges. Quite a few have told me that the principles we follow have helped them develop a new perspective on life and have helped them function better. That means that we may have touched as many as fifty-five thousand employees in different ways. If the new generation of managers takes up these ideas, we can certainly influence many more thousands, perhaps hundreds of thousands. That's a big presumption, I know, but so was EFCS when we first talked about it.

Each year, a few hundred people leave HCLT to join other companies or to follow different paths in their lives. I consider these people alumni of the EFCS school of thought, and I hope that they, too, will take our ideas with them to their new endeavors. I hope they will be alert to the nature of the value zone in their new situation and be aware of the distribution of power there as well as be conscious of how accountabilities add value or create obstructions. Above all, I hope, they will be motivated to turn conventional management wisdom upside down.

We know that a single good thought can change society for the better. I believe that ours is a good thought.

When we started this journey, our goal was to transform HCLT, and after five years of travel, we have certainly done so. For me, it has been a humbling experience of self-discovery, one that I could not have undertaken alone. People throughout the company had ideas that would never otherwise have occurred to me. They have put the concepts into practice in ways that amazed and delighted me. They regularly revealed new horizons, the mountains beyond the mountains, that I did not see.

This is truly a book with fifty-five thousand authors.

Our journey transformed not only our company— but transformed me, as well. In 2005, when we began, it was as if I was blind, groping my way forward. I wish I could say that I saw the path clearly back then, but I did not. I am glad that I took the uncharted journey because that has been the fun of it.

Today, as much as my eyes have been opened, I wonder if I am still in the dark. A few years from now, will I look back at 2010 and say again that I was blind and just groping my way forward?

Notes

Chapter Two

1. Andy McCue, "Dixons Outsources IT to India in US$263M Deal," *ZDNet Asia*, January 23, 2006, www.zdnetasia.com/news/business/0,39044229,39306969,00.htm.

2. "HCL Ties Up with DSG International," *EFYTimes*, January 19, 2006.

3. "HCL, Teradyne of US in $70-M Outsourcing Deal," *Hindu Business Line*, July 14, 2006, www.thehindubusinessline.com/2006/07/14/stories/2006071405150100.htm.

4. McCue, "Dixons Outsources IT to India."

5. Barry Rubenstein, "HCL Technologies Is Disruptive and Bears Watching," IDC Event Flash, November 2006.

6. "Hungry Tiger, Dancing Elephant: How India Is Changing IBM's World," *The Economist*, April 4, 2007.

Chapter Three

1. C. K. Prahalad, *The Fortune at the Bottom of the Pyramid: Eradicating Poverty Through Profits* (Upper Saddle River, NJ: Wharton School Publishing, 2005).

Chapter Four

1. Ori Brafman and Rod A. Beckstrom, *The Starfish and the Spider: The Unstoppable Power of Leaderless Organizations* (New York: Portfolio, 2006); and Rod A. Beckstrom, "The Starfish and the

Spider," The Rod Beckstrom Group, Web page, April 26, 2009, www.beckstrom.com/The_Starfish_and_The_Spider.

Chapter Five

1. Gary Hamel and C. K. Prahalad, "Strategic Intent," *Harvard Business Review*, July-August 2005, http://hbr.org/2005/07/strategic-intent/ar/1.

Acknowledgments

First and foremost, I would like to thank the fifty-five thousand wonderful partners and coauthors of this book: the HCLites. Without your ideas, your belief in what we were doing, and your indulging us in some initiatives that many might have considered crazy, *Employees First, Customers Second* would never have become a reality. The members of my leadership team, you who dared to walk a path very few have walked before, are the true heroes of this transformation. Each of you is a fascinating person who has taught me so much; I walk shoulder to shoulder with you with great pride. I would also like to acknowledge all the former HCLites, because this journey would have been impossible without the foundations you laid over a thirty-year period; your footprints have guided us toward new destinations and firmer ground.

Shiv Nadar, you have been a wonderful friend, guide, and mentor. You inspired me as you have inspired so many other people. Your spirit—to experiment and to push the boundaries—is what I treasure the most. Thank you for believing in me.

To my customers and partners, some of whom have become friends, thank you for believing in us from the earliest days of our journey. It has been your support and participation that have helped us to evolve and improve EFCS with each passing year. You have been enthusiastic supporters of our strategy and your desire for us to succeed has been the fundamental reason that EFCS lives and breathes today.

To my industry peers, thank you for being an inspiration. You challenged us to compete harder every day, and that is why the journey has been so much fun. We have learned a great deal from each other, and I hope that we continue this competition that is based on ideas and values.

In true EFCS fashion, I have relied on friends and colleagues to help me create this book. I had the passion, if not the skills, to write a book that would be worth reading, so I looked to others to realize a dream that sometimes seemed impossible to make a reality. Many thanks to Zulfia and Amrita, two bright sparks, who helped me conduct research and translate ideas into words, and to Meena, who managed the process and ensured we kept walking the path. Thanks to Suresh, Krishnan, Heena, R. Anand, Neha, and Anand Pillai for helping me think through the structure and format of the book. Thanks to many others in my leadership team for reviewing the drafts and giving valuable input. Without your help and participation, I probably would have given up.

The spaces between the notes are where music is made and I'm grateful that I had my composer, John Butman, to bring music to this book. I never thought that words could speak what I feel until I met John. Thank you to Jacque Murphy, my editor at Harvard Business Press, for her astute feedback and for keeping me on course. My thanks to David Wan, CEO of Harvard Business Publishing, for suggesting I write this book in the first place and for his support throughout the process. Thanks also to Linda A. Hill and Tarun Khanna, who coauthored the Harvard Business School case study that laid the foundation for the book.

It takes a village to make a man and perhaps a good-sized town to make an author. My mother inspired me to fight all odds. "Difficult is nothing," she would say. "It is just different." This book is dedicated to her because it is her spirit that breathes life into me every morning. My father, during the evening walks we enjoyed together, instilled in me the desire to think big and to act with integrity. My wife, Anupama, is my closest friend and the woman behind my success and strength. Thank you to my brothers, Neeraj and Vibhu, who are my biggest supporters and critics. Their comments on the manuscript were very valuable. Thanks to my Aunt Kailash for instilling pride in me—pride for our history and pride as the way to live life. To my children, Varun and Sophiyaa, thanks for teaching me what love and Gen Y are all about. And I am grateful to so many other friends and members of my family who helped to make me the person I am today.

My special thanks to my team and the children who work with me in our charitable organization Sampark, which has a vision of creating "a million smiles" by helping to improve the quality of education in India; all of my proceeds from this book will go to Sampark.

It takes courage to walk a different path, but when you do, you discover that you are not alone; there are many who wish to walk with you. I acknowledge all who believe in walking different paths. It's the act of walking and not the success at the end that makes the walk worth it.

Finally, thank you to all the readers who picked up this book and delved into its contents. I wish you the best in your journey.

Index

About the Author

VINEET NAYAR is chief executive officer of HCL Technologies, Ltd. (HCLT), one of India's fastest-growing global information technology services company.

Vineet joined HCL in 1985 after earning his MBA from XLRI. In 1993, he created the start-up company Comnet, where he developed and put into practice many of the ideas that are described in this book.

In 2005, he became president and then, in 2007, the CEO of HCL Technologies, where over the next five years, he led a remarkable turnaround. HCLT has become one of the Indian IT stars, recognized around the world for its business performance and its innovative and transformative management practices.

In 2009, HCLT was named the Number One Best Employer in India and one of the top twenty-five Best Employers in Asia by Hewitt Associates, and *BusinessWeek* listed HCLT as one of the five emerging companies in the world to watch.